THE ICEMAN

MAINSTREAM *SPORT*

THE ICEMAN

THE STORY OF THE MOST SUCCESSFUL RUGBY LEAGUE COACH EVER

JOHN MONIE WITH TOM MATHER

EDINBURGH AND LONDON

First published in Great Britain in 2001 by
MAINSTREAM PUBLISHING COMPANY (EDINBURGH) LTD
7 Albany Street
Edinburgh EH1 3UG

ISBN 1 84018 671 2

This edition, 2002

A catalogue record for this book is available from the British Library

Typeset in Stone
Printed and bound in Great Britain by
Cox & Wyman Ltd

CONTENTS

Most coaches get the sack. How long can you coach before getting the sack?

– John Monie

FOREWORD

I first met John Monie at a National Rugby League Coaching Camp in the early 1980s. We were both on the coaching staff. I was coaching at South Brisbane and he was the first-grade coach at Parramatta.

Looking back, we were both young and neither of us had any idea of the twists and turns that lay ahead of us. We became friends immediately. He is an easy guy to like. He is laid back (not about his coaching), has a relaxed manner, does not take himself too seriously and is not opinionated. To sum it up, he is a good bloke.

We both had great expectations and we knew how we wanted to coach. John is a realist, and one of the things that struck me with him was he knew where he was going. He knew himself well and there would be no shortcuts to his success. John played a little football in Sydney, but it was in the bush that he did most of his playing and coaching. What he learned was how to handle teams and to get the best out of the individuals he was playing with. Those playing and coaching years in the NSW country were the bricks and mortar of his later coaching successes. John has never been full of himself nor has he been a self-promoter. He has a confidence that only someone who is at peace with himself can enjoy.

Since we first met, a lot of water – some of it a trifle muddy – has passed under the bridge. The face of the game has changed dramatically, but one thing that has not changed in twenty years is the strength of our friendship. There is mutual respect between us, and I regard our friendship very highly. We coached against each other on numerous occasions: Broncos v Parramatta, Broncos v Auckland, Broncos v Wigan, Canberra Raiders v Parramatta. Generally before the match we would have a game of tennis and spend some time together and I would always enjoy his company. From my point of view, there was no celebration after the match if you happened to win. You knew it was your job but there was no personal satisfaction, and if you lost you felt it was okay to lose to him. Looking back, I don't think we had anything to prove to each other because of our friendship and of our confidence in ourselves.

Often in coaching you find yourself out there on your own. It is a natural instinct that you support your players and your club and often you'll upset the opposition camp and their coach. Strong friendships with other coaches are a rarity, and that is why I consider our long-standing association unique.

John produced a brand of football with his teams that was good to watch. His teams were always disciplined and they played the game in the spirit that it was meant to be played. He was never guilty of over-coaching and, in my opinion, he always seemed to have the timing right in the preparation of his teams.

He and I have similar mentors – Jack Gibson and Ron Massey. They were both people whose opinions we trusted and in whom we confided. John coached the second grade under Jack, and when big Jack retired at the end of 1983 he merely told the committee not to look for a replacement. 'The man for the job is already here,' said Jack. That man was John. Ron and Jack were men of few words but when they said something you listened. They were the two men who had a huge influence on both of us.

While John won a premiership at Parramatta and coaching stints with the Auckland Warriors and London Broncos, there is no doubt that his trademark success was at Wigan. From 1989 to 1994 he achieved unprecedented triumph with that champion English club. They won every conceivable trophy on offer and he was named English Coach of the Year four times. His achievements in winning premierships in Australia and England were outstanding. He was adored by the Wigan fans and I know it was a very happy time in his life. I'm not sure if he is rated as the finest coach they have ever had in England, but his record says he should be. I believe one of his greatest achievements, though, has been his own personal growth. He once mentioned that if they had had a competition at school on who was most likely to fail, the teachers would certainly have put him in the final. But somewhere from that background he rose to conquer in one of the toughest jobs – coaching. But, most importantly, he wasn't just a coach, he was one of the best.

John is now retired – or so he says – and has once again shown just how astute he is by moving to Queensland to live. No doubt he will continue to dabble in the game to which he has contributed so greatly – first as a player and, second, as a coach for the past forty years. But I'm sure that John is grateful for the opportunities and the great moments that have been presented to him through his association with rugby league. He is a much better person for the experience and so are the hundreds of young men who were fortunate to have been coached by him. I am looking forward to his company on the benches at the Broncos' home games.

I am also grateful to the Australian journalist and writer Les Wilson for writing the final chapter in the book, but not nessecarily in the John Monie story.

Wayne Bennett

PREFACE TO THE 2002 EDITION

There are many reasons why this book was written, not least for rugby fans the world over. Professional sport by its very nature is a hard and cruel world at times. It seems to me that Rugby League has a particular weakness, that of quickly forgetting its heroes! Be they player or coach, the attitude seems to be you are only as good as your last match. Once players and coaches finish in the sport they are quickly forgotten – not the case in other sports. Such players and coaches seem to become revered and the reverence increases as time passes. Knighthoods are bestowed on sporting 'greats' – in Rugby League brickbats are thrown at them. John Monie revolutionised the British game and yet was allowed to fade out of the game in this country without so much as a by your leave. Perhaps the time has come to eulogise about this game's great stars. This book is a humble attempt to do just that. To honour a man who gave a lifetime to the game and was successful on both sides of the globe.

My thanks go first to John for the many hours he spent talking with me about his work, something he is not prone to do. To Julie, his wife, for the many occasions she prompted his memory or told me the real story, John being too modest to say just what his role had been. My thanks also to Les Wilson for working with John in Australia to produce the last epilogue. Finally, last but by no means least, to Hilary who spent hours reading the original drafts and helped get them into the shape the reader now sees. I suppose in all honesty the thanks should really go to all those players who responded to John Monie's coaching to such an extent that he became probably the greatest coach in the game. Thus causing this book to see the light of day.

Tom Mather

1

INTRODUCTION

'Have the courage to confound expectations.'

Most sporting pundits would agree that the game of rugby league is probably the toughest sport in the world to play. Consequently, people have a picture in their mind of the typical rugby player who is capable of playing the game: big, burly, lacking somewhat in verbal dexterity, generally speaking a pair of hands the size of muck shovels, not to mention ears of a similar size and cauliflower in appearance, shoulders that make one think that the coat-hanger has not been removed before the wearer donned the jacket!

John Monie does not fit into any one of those categories. Retired jockey maybe, but rugby player never. At around 5 feet 5 inches in height and almost as wide, with hair tinged grey by time, this neat, dapper man conveys an air of quiet calm tranquillity. When he talks, there is a twinkle of mischief in his eyes. He speaks with a quiet gentle voice that belies his chosen profession. For this is the man who is probably the most successful rugby league coach in the English game's history of over one hundred years.

You could be forgiven for asking the question, how does he

manage to control, rule, cajole men of seventeen or eighteen stones who are over six feet tall? Yet he has done it more successfully than any other coach the game has seen. He has been successful not only in England with the world-famous Wigan club, but also with Parramatta down under and the fledgling Auckland Warriors in New Zealand. To be in his company is to realise just how he has managed to be so successful. Start to talk rugby with Monie, or, as he prefers to call it, 'footy', and you see the twinkle quickly fade from his eyes. It is replaced by a steely glint and fierce determination. When he talks footy he is attending to business, and business demands one's full and undivided attention. There is no room for compromise in rugby league, not in Monie's opinion anyway.

To give you some idea of just how determined he is as a coach, one need only look to an incident with his own son Stephen, who was once playing in a team coached by Monie. When the youngster dislocated a shoulder in a tackle, Monie simply called for him to be removed and a substitute to be placed on the field. It was not until the match was over that Monie the coach was replaced by Monie the father. Up to that moment his whole concentration had been absorbed by the job in hand, that of winning a 'footy' match, and watching the boys play. Once it was over he became a concerned parent. He waited until the game was over, then went to see how Stephen was.

He talks with a passion about the game, he understands its demands, not only on the players but also on coaches. He can unravel a game plan put together by an opposition coach quicker than anyone else. This is the skill that at times has pulled games out of the fire while he was coaching Wigan in their glory years. I observed it on a cold wet Thursday night at Post Office Road, Featherstone.

It was only a reserve grade match and he was there simply to run his eye over some of the youngsters playing in the Wigan reserve team. Within five minutes he was actually calling each play the opposition ran in their set of six tackles. The uncanny thing was he did it with unerring accuracy. It was this talent that allowed him to anticipate the game plan that Bradford would adopt against Wigan in a Challenge Cup semi-final. He simply put together his own game strategy to counter Bradford, the result a 71 points to 10 win, and this in a semi-final tie! It is a record score which stands to this day. In all probability it will never be bettered. Monie had cut through the tension, unravelled the Bradford game plan, shown his players what they had to do to win the match and coached them to do just that. The ruthlessness displayed that afternoon by both coach and team was awesome, to say the least. Bradford were swept away with not a hint of compassion. He was, though, equally ruthless with his own players! After that historic match, the players came into training to be greeted with a video session of edited segments of the game. Not, though, what the players had expected; the video contained every mistake the Wigan team had made during the match. Every missed tackle, every dropped ball, every error was in the edited lowlights. It was his way of bringing them down to earth again, making sure they concentrated on the job in hand, which was simply to prepare to win the next game!

By his own admission, it could all have turned out so very differently in those early days at the Central Park club. Then perhaps this book would not have needed to be written! In his first season at Wigan in the first round of the Challenge Cup Wigan were drawn to play Hull KR at Hull. The match was played in a freezing, howling gale which blew straight off the North Sea and down the pitch. Wigan held a slim lead of only two points in the second half but faced the full force of the gale in that second stanza. It was then that potential disaster struck, when Joe Lydon, the full-back, had to leave the field, having damaged his Acromio-clavicular joint in a shoulder.

With Lydon off the field, Wigan had lost their field kicker. There was literally no one on the team who could kick the ball strongly enough to get the team out of the defensive stranglehold Hull KR were imposing with the help of the strong wind. Hull KR were camped in the Wigan 22-metre zone with no way for Wigan to get out in their set of six tackles. As Monie said, 'Ged Byrne was struggling to kick the ball more than twenty metres up field, so Wigan were always on the defensive. In the end I got on the radio and spoke to Joe and pointed out to him he did not kick with his shoulder. I told him to get back on the field and if he did nothing else just simply kick us into better field position. He could kick hard and low under the wind and at least get us out of the danger area.'

Joe Lydon duly obliged. In spite of the pain he returned to the action, nursed his shoulder and managed to kick Wigan out of the defensive hole they were in. The remainder of the game was played out in the comparative safety zone of the halfway line. Wigan went on to secure a victory in the match by 8 points to 6, going on to win the cup that season.

It launched the spectacular reign of John Monie, a reign which saw unprecedented success for the club. However, as he is the first to admit, it could have been very different had that first-round tie gone against the club, as it could so easily have done. Who knows just what would have happened to that great team and their coach? It is on such little things that reputations can be won or lost. Luckily for Monie and the game, he won! Monie could always win the tight games, especially in the 1980s and 1990s. The rest, as they say, is history.

John Huxley, the present media and public relations manager for the Rugby Football League, has little doubt about Monie's place in the history of the game: 'At some time in the future, when historians look back on the game, then Monie's effect on our game here in England will be seen for what it really is – dramatic.'

Huxley's reason for thinking this way is quite clear: 'It was Monie in his first spell at Wigan who brought us into the era of full-time professional players. Graeme Lowe had begun the process, but it was Monie who drove it home. He was the consummate professional who needed to work full time with players in order to prepare them in a manner which was acceptable to him.' John Huxley believes that during his early stint at Wigan, Monie took the club so far ahead of the rest of the English game, it took a decade for it to catch up with him.

Huxley, prior to moving to Rugby League Headquarters, was a well-respected journalist, so was able to experience Monie from two standpoints. Wearing his reporter's hat, he felt, 'In Monie's first spell at Wigan the universal respect he commanded was breathtaking to behold, and not only from his own players, I can tell you. The other thing he did was to introduce the English journalists to a friendly, knowledgeable and enjoyable media experience. He was always approachable.'

As for Monie's finest achievement, Huxley, quite controversially, it could be argued, suggested it came after he left the club at the end of his first time at Wigan.

'Winning the World Club Championship in 1995 down under in Brisbane. I always felt that the team which won was still *his* team. Mind you, the demolition of Bradford in that cup semi-final would run it close. Bradford were no mugs, but the way Wigan took them apart was the most awesome display of rugby I have ever seen anywhere. Either here or down under. No team would have lived with them that day.'

What makes players play for Monie is, simply, respect. They respect his knowledge, honesty and integrity, but more importantly they respect him as a man. Not only has he coached successfully at the highest level, but he has also played at the highest level. He knows what players are feeling, what their worries are. He has the ability to understand players as individuals who need to be coaxed and cajoled, and sometimes, to put it bluntly, need a 'rollicking' to make them perform. Equally importantly, he never loses his cool. The half-time dressing-room is not a place for ranting and raving. All that does is cause players to lose respect for a coach. If they are doing things wrong, players are professional enough to know it. There is no need to state the obvious.

They need to know what they are doing wrong and what they have to do to put it right. Monie always seemed to be able to put his finger on the problem and, more importantly, he seemed to be able to come up with a solution. Certainly, his teams have won far more games than they have lost!

Immediately after the match is also not the time to praise or chastise players. That is better done in the cold light of day after studying the match video. In the heat of the match it is so easy to make a mistake, criticise the wrong player for an error he did not make, or praise the wrong player. Better to wait and watch the match video coldly and dispassionately. Monie knows that, as do the players who have performed for him over the years. That is why they respect him. Mind you, it could simply be that he gets them winning money more often than losing money!

Another anomaly about Monie is that he also understands the business side of the game. It is a quality not all coaches have. All too often coaches see only the playing side of things; they have no wish to know or understand the commercial aspects of running a rugby club. For them, it is simple. If they need a player they should be allowed to sign a player. If they wish to transfer a player, they should be allowed to do so. All that matters to them is getting a team on the park on match days. Monie appreciates that occasionally it is just a little more complicated than that.

Sometimes it just makes good business sense to offload a player who may well have another season or two in him. Sense that is, if the price is right for the club and there is a youngster ready to step in and replace the leaving player. He did it while at Wigan when Ellery Hanley was allowed to leave the club for his home-town club, Leeds. Many thought Hanley was irreplaceable and that the team would disintegrate once he left. Monie knew better! He had a youngster who was bursting for a first-team spot. That player was Phil Clarke, who came in, filled Hanley's boots, and the team simply carried on winning.

What is not good sense as far as he is concerned is what happened to him one closed season. While in Australia, he learned that his chairman had sold his international scrum-half and bought a reserve-grade replacement from another club. Although he wasn't pleased, he simply got on with the job of coaching the squad to a cup and league double once again. Without any histrionics, he would simply assess the new player's strengths and weaknesses, work on eliminating the weakness and improving the strengths. He would work out how best to use the newcomer in the existing scheme of things and get on with the job of winning footy matches.

He does care about his players, although it does not seem so apparent at times. When John Clarke, the young Wigan hooker, was jailed on an assault charge, it was Monie who contacted the local prison where Clarke was serving his sentence to ask if the club could use the gym facilities. 'Oh, and by the way, would it be possible for young Clarke to train with the boys?' It was Monie's way of telling Clarke that they had not forgotten him. Also it made sure the hooker stayed in contact with his team-mates.

Having arranged it, Monie simply got on with the job, no song and dance, no publicity about the matter, no blowing his own trumpet – that is not his style! Furthermore, it was not a great surprise that when Monie wanted the youngster to move to London Broncos there was no hesitation: Clarke just signed the contract as quickly as he could!

Monie is, though, a coach who is photogenic and, along with his communication skills, it has made him a favourite with the media. Both the BBC and Sky TV are keen to acquire his services. Not only does he look good on the box, he actually talks sense! Monie can articulate about the game in a unique manner, he is not patronising to the knowledgeable fans and does not baffle the casual watcher with jargon. He seems capable of saying in a sentence what others need a page to convey. He is television's dream come true.

The BBC rugby commentator Ray French considers Monie to be one of the best summarisers around: 'What makes him so is his honesty and integrity. Also he can grasp what is happening in a game so early that he can tell you how a match is going to unfold, or how play will develop. I suppose that comes from his coaching experience. He picks up incidents which occur in a game and can then encapsulate them clearly and precisely for the viewers.'

The other thing Ray French likes about Monie is his fairness; he is not one for castigating players who make mistakes during a match: 'John always looks positively at players, pointing out the problems which lead up to mistakes being made. That is not easy, and what the viewers don't realise also is just how difficult it is to summarise an instant replay. John is the coolest man I have seen in such situations. He quickly spots what is important and then articulates on it as if it has been scripted, which of course it has not. The replays come at you so quickly you cannot script anything.' French sums him up in a word: professional. 'You need to have a rapport with your summariser, and respect for him. John commands both: he is the ultimate professional, either as a coach or as a TV commentator.' Monie is equally at home with the members of the press. They like him simply because he gives them good copy. No one-liners from Monie; if asked a question he will articulate on the merits or otherwise of the question, although don't expect him to be critical of a match official, that is not his style. In all probability if, after studying the match video, he feels strongly about some decision which went against his team, then it is the controller of referees who will get the benefit of some well-chosen words. Like many in the game, he feels that such matters are best handled in-house, as it were.

It must also be said that Monie sees relationships with the press as just that, relationships. Martin Sadler, editor of the *League Express* newspaper, is one journalist who has had many conversations with Monie and considered him to be a 'thoughtful coach' but one who was not forthcoming. Not forthcoming, that is, until you had gained his trust. As Sadler said: 'He has always struck me as a quiet operator, not one to blow his own trumpet. He will, though, be remembered at Wigan for all the trophies he has won.' However, these, funnily enough, according to Sadler, were not his greatest achievements. 'For me, it was the way he put together a team, and a team with massive egos, egos which were at times rather fragile. People like Gregory, Edwards and, of course, Hanley. John Monie actually managed to mould such players into a team, and also developed a team ethos among them. For that, I feel he wasn't, and still has not been, given the credit he deserves.'

Sadler also felt that perhaps his winning of the inaugural grand final during his second stint at the Wigan club was as good as anything he ever achieved in his first four-year spell with them: 'For me the measure of a coach is simple. If you can go to a club and make a noticeable difference to that club, then you can justifiably be called a good coach.'

It is that theme which is echoed by Dave Hadfield, the rugby league correspondent for the *Independent* newspaper: 'I feel that in his first spell at Wigan, when his ideas were new to the country, he was sensational. I don't think I have seen any man handle a club side as well as he did. When you think of the monumental personalities he had to handle, his achievements were astonishing.' Hadfield felt that the Wigan of Monie's first spell was the proverbial 'well-oiled machine'. As he put it, 'They never seemed to have any troughs, or attacks of the vapours, which would see them lose two or three matches on the trot. It was the very high level of consistency that he brought to the club which was outstanding. While there is no one match which was a stand-out in my mind, I think his greatest achievement was winning the championship when they were forced to play matches almost every other day as the 1991–92 season came to a close. They also went on to win the Challenge Cup as well!'

Like many, Hadfield thought Monie was a journalist's dream, although he did suggest that Monie had a bit of a reputation for being difficult to extract information from: 'I never found that, quite the opposite in fact. He was interesting and open and was a gifted communicator. He could illuminate the game, the players, how the players fitted into situations and so on. Also, he had good man-management skills.'

Hadfield argued that Monie's management skills were honed by the master of such matters, Aussie coach Jack Gibson, who had been his guru at Parramatta.

> I would say it was little use any player going in to see John Monie and complaining he was not getting a fair crack of the whip. John would have the facts at his fingertips: tackles made, tackles missed, hit-ups in each half, contribution to the team's effort – all would be carefully logged away. He, like Gibson, has the ability to get under the skin of a player, to understand how he operates, what makes him tick. He was, and still is, a master at blooding new young players into a squad and getting just one more very good season out of a player at the end of his career.

The only blot on the Monie career, according to Hadfield, was the time at Auckland Warriors: 'It never really worked for him down there, for whatever reason, but then perhaps we are judging him against the very high standards he achieved at Parramatta and Wigan, two old-established clubs.' Certainly, the Warriors were not enormously successful under Monie, but then again they have not been successful since he left them!

There is much more to Monie than the winning of trophies. They are the end-product as far as he is concerned. It is his simple belief that if you get everything right at a club, players, support staff and so on, then the trophies will come as a matter of course. There are two maxims which seem to rule his thinking. First, a good 'big un' will always beat a good 'little un'. Nothing new in that I suppose. Second, a good old player will generally do better than a young player. Please do not get him wrong; he does not believe that old players are better than young players, rather that they make fewer mistakes in a game.

It is those mistakes which can cost you a match. Monie prefers to blood a young player into his system. He likes to choose his games carefully to ensure the pressure is not too great for a youngster. Like any coach, he prefers to be in control of, rather than be controlled by external forces. By blooding youngsters carefully, he ensures that the seasoned players will have enough time to look after the kids during the match. They will not be allowed to develop 'bad habits', as it were, because the rest of the team were under pressure and unable to offer assistance or guidance as the game was in progress. One seasoned professional player told me that when he was just breaking into Monie's first-team squad he received invaluable help from the incomparable Aussie centre Gene Miles.

> The pace is breathtaking when you first play first-grade rugby, and I remember Miles talking to me all through the game. He asked if I was tired, which was a little silly really as I must have looked absolutely knackered, mid-way through the second half of the game. It was then he said, 'First rule: take a breather when we are on the attack; you can simply drop out of the line. Never, never, take a rest on defence. Remember, we will get the ball back, that will give you the chance to get a rest.' It was advice I never forgot, and it is a practice I still use today. Now I find myself telling the young players the same thing.

That is why Monie likes to pick and choose when to play young players. He is, and always has been, a thinker about the game, and, surprisingly to some, is also an innovator. During his time at Parramatta he brought a dietician into the club, feeling it might well give his team an edge. This was at a time when the game was still serving steak and eggs to its players for the pre-match lunch. These days the players' diet is much more controlled with protein- and carbohydrate-loading. Pasta and cake or chicken and fish are the order of the day, not so back in the 1970s. At that time the 'in thing' was buckwheat, which was the pasta equivalent of the day. The dietician gave bags of buckwheat to the players with instructions to use it in place of normal flour. After a month or so, Monie asked his players what they thought of the diet and the buckwheat. Peter Sterling took him to the front entrance of the ground and asked him to look at what the pigeons were doing and how they looked!

'Look,' said Sterling, 'have you ever seen pigeons with chests like that? Look at the condition of those feathers, coach. They must be the fittest pigeons in Sydney!'

Monie got the message. The following day he fired the dietician. He had, though, given it a go, as they say down under. The players, unfortunately, were not prepared to, and had been throwing the buckwheat to the birds on the way out to their cars after training. No change for them in their diet. No, they would carry on eating what they had always eaten. Mind you, they had good reason to: it got them to two grand finals. (Or was it five – three with Jack Gibson and two with Monie?)

The strange thing is that when Monie first arrived at Wigan, he came with a reputation as a coach who was strong on defence. It is a fact that people tend to forget, given the way the Wigan team used to play. It is a tag he is very proud of. It has always been his view that defence wins football games. If you stop the opposition scoring and don't score yourself, then you gain a draw. On the other hand, if you can manage a score you win the game. Whenever things have not been going well on the field, wherever he has been coaching, his immediate reaction is simple and unvarying. Cut out all the fancy stuff, work hard all week on defence, play a simple game plan and execute it. By doing that, he believes the players will regain confidence in themselves and their team-mates. They will regain confidence in the game plan, and once that confidence returns so will the 'fancy stuff'.

When you see some of the performances his Wigan teams have given him, it is hard to believe it is based on defence. In a championship semi-final they ran a Leeds team off the Central Park pitch. Martin Offiah actually crossed for *ten* tries in the match, a club record at the time.

Monie's is a story of great achievement within his chosen sport, not only as a player but also as a coach. However, it is a story that has its highs as well as its lows. The highs, generally speaking, have occurred when he has been in control of given situations. The lows have come when other people have been in control of Monie's destiny. He left Wigan the first time on a high, having swept the board of trophies, as it were. He was in control, he knew he was going, he had engineered it, he controlled when he would leave. He left Auckland because people within the club decided they wanted to remove him. The reasons for that decision were many perhaps, but Monie had little control over them. He simply wanted what was best for Auckland, and if that meant more Aussie players when the controlling influences at the club felt they wanted more Kiwi players, then more Aussies it would be. Monie was not prepared to compromise in matters of football policy.

The second occasion he left Wigan, he left because other people wanted it to happen. Ironically, when Wigan sacked him the club did not win a trophy that year, the first time for some fifteen years they had been without such a success. Monie felt that had he not been sacked, there was every chance that the club could have won the grand final a second time.

It was, though, not to be, and Monie, as he always does, went away, assessed the situation, and decided he still had a couple of good years of coaching in him. He sat back and waited for clubs to approach him, and eventually it was London Broncos who gave him the head-coach role he enjoys. Sadly, three games from the end of that first season, working with a squad he had inherited and with only five wins, the directors felt the way forward was to sack the coach again! Monie was the fourth coach to be sacked by the club in two years. Now it seems he is destined to return to Australia and a quiet retirement from the game he has graced all his life, although I think television may be able to lure him away from that.

Monie is unique in that he is a players' coach. It is they who are important to him. He does seem to be able to balance that against the need to keep a club financially sound. He understands that at times the chairman has his own agenda and because he is looking at a broader picture it sometimes appears players are being sacrificed when in truth it is good sound business sense to let the player go or not to bring a player to the club.

This book is an attempt to put into the public domain the career of John Monie, both in the UK and in Australia, with the Parramatta club, and across the Tasman Sea in Auckland. Then readers will see for themselves the events that have influenced and been influenced by truly the most successful coach of rugby league football the game has ever seen.

2

EARLY DAYS

'Do your job – if everyone does their job,
then a little bit extra, we will win!'

John Monie is a product of the state of New South Wales, in particular the Central Coast, an area about an hour north of Sydney by car. It was inevitable then that he, like most Australian youngsters brought up near the ocean, would develop two sporting loves, 'footy' and surfing. In his case, surprisingly enough, for a time his first love became surfing!

As a kid growing up, he was able to enjoy both. It must be said that he made his mark in both sports from an early age. By the time he was seventeen, however, he had broken into the local team, Woy-Woy. He played stand-off or five-eight, as the Aussies refer to it. He broke into a very strong junior side and made rapid progress. During that season of 1967 he represented the Southern Division side, his first representative honour.

He made his mark in the game as a player quite quickly and impressed the people in the know enough to persuade the relatively new Cronulla club to give him a contract. Once at Cronulla, he quickly made the number-six jumper his own, taking over from Jack Danzey after a handful of reserve-grade appearances. We are, though, jumping the gun a little; it may be better to begin at the beginning.

As was said earlier, Monie is a product of Woy-Woy, which is almost equidistant between Sydney to the south and Newcastle to the north. There is an expressway which connects those two cities and the so-called Central Coast is that strip between the expressway and the ocean. It is an area rich in rugby league tradition and, for that matter, rugby league clubs. As Monie remembered: 'The Central Coast has a very strong rugby league history. There were, I think, eight first-grade clubs; maybe five of those had got their own "leagues" club, which means, in effect, they virtually own their own grounds. Each club had first grade, second grade, third grade, under-eighteen, under-sixteen, all the way back to under-five!'

It was at under-six level that the young Monie began his rugby-playing career, but not with Woy-Woy, rather it was the unusually named Scone that first saw his talent. Scone was a town in the Hunter Valley, famed more for its wine and thoroughbred horses than its 'footy' players. It was the latter which Monie's grandfather and uncles worked in, training those thoroughbreds.

Monie played rugby all the way through school in Scone, as he recalled:

> The secondary school and the primary school up at Scone were on the same site. I can remember that I was in sixth class, which then was the last year of primary school before you went into secondary. I thought I was very lucky because I used to get two days of sport. I could play rugby league for the secondary school on a Thursday and I would go back to the primary school on Friday and represent them! While I was at the primary school I was lucky enough and good enough to be able to represent the older secondary school.

It was at the age of fourteen that his family moved back to the coast to a place called Ocean Beach, which was close to Woy-Woy.

Here, the schooling continued, as did the rugby. Now he was also playing club rugby for Woy-Woy. He played during the week for school and at the weekend he played for his club, which was the way most youngsters operated. It was then that a rival sport attracted the attention of the youngster, namely surfing. He is the first to admit that his sporting career could have taken a totally different direction:

> Rugby league was what I always wanted to do until I moved to the coast. Then I found the more time I spent in the water surfing, the more it grabbed me. You have to remember that surfing is more of a lifestyle really than a sport. It became part of my lifestyle at that time. I did, though, in the end manage to combine the two.
>
> In those early days when you came out of the age divisions for your club, you progressed up the grades. The under-sixteen age division was known as D grade. Once I left D grade I moved up to C grade, which was under-eighteen. That would be around 1965. I only played C grade for about a half of that first season and was actually at the end of that season playing for the Woy-Woy first-grade team. They, at that time, were having an undefeated season, so I went from the junior side in the club to first grade, playing five-eight. That side was a very good side, and ended up winning the competition and, as I said, went through the season undefeated.

This was at a time when Monie was still only seventeen. It was a feat which did not go unnoticed. It was not only the professional clubs that began to take an interest in this little five-eight. Representative honours in this 'country' football system were to follow.

> What used to happen back then was that all the country

areas in NSW were divided into divisions. Strangely enough Central Coast, which was between Sydney and Newcastle, was classified as being part of Southern Division, which was actually on the other side of Sydney! The Wollongong side of the city. At that time Newcastle did not have a side in the competition, it had its own comp which was very strong, so my Central Coast group joined with teams south of the city in this Southern Division. In my second season I ended up playing for those Southern Division sides which were the representative sides. From there I was picked up by the Cronulla people. The scouts for the Sydney clubs always scouted those country championships as they were called then. I got an offer which I think came to me via the Woy-Woy club.

The funny thing was that in those country finals I actually kicked a field goal from a long way out! I have never been much of a kicker anyway, but I happened to hit this one as good as you could hit them, and they were worth two points then. Perhaps it was that which tipped it in my direction. The other guy who got picked up from Southern Division was Tony Branston, who went to St George. Tony also got into the country side, which was a representative side selected from the country championships. The country side used to play the city side every season, and Tony Branston played five-eight for 'country'. The following year, while at St George, he went on tour with the Kangaroos as the Aussie five-eight!

It is interesting to note that in those seemingly far-off days youngsters who were signed from the country were invariably put up in digs close to the stadium. Given the vastness of Australia, you could not expect youngsters to travel into Sydney from the 'country' areas to train for the clubs. Better to get them into the city on a permanent basis so they could concentrate on simply playing rugby league.

When a club signed a country player, they used to lodge them with a family. I moved in with a butcher by the name of Ron Fuzz. I lived with him and his wife Betty. He was the local butcher at a place called Ingadene just south of Southerland in the Cronulla St George area. The club was actually called Cronulla Southerland when I signed for them.

Signing for them was pretty handy for me as it allowed me to get a lot of surfing in! I could get down to the south coast, and I also got to know some good surf spots around Cronulla. At the time I was shaping surfboards as well. That was my job outside rugby league. I had been working shaping boards up on the Central Coast. When I got to Cronulla in the second season I got a job with Gordon and Smith Surfboards on Tarrenpoint Road. So I put my time in there, shaped a few boards a week, and got plenty of time in the surf riding them.

We played on the Sunday and then Monday was always up at the hospital with the physio and that sort of thing. As it was an off day, everybody would gather for a drink in the afternoon. Tuesday saw us back into it. I still found time to get in the ocean with the surfboard.

It did not take the young Monie long to make his mark at first grade in the Sydney comp. In fact he reckoned he made his mark even before the competition got under way:

I was very lucky, Cronulla was one of the new clubs. The season before I arrived the five-eight was a guy called Jack Danzey, who went on to be a referee in Sydney when he retired from playing. Halfway through pre-season training he decided to retire. Whether I had out-trained him or not, I don't know; I was very fit in those days because I spent all my time either training or surfing. I was as fit as you could be and I had a real good pre-season. Jack retired, as I said, which was great for me. I went straight into first grade and spent three seasons with the club. I played around eighty first-grade and five or six reserve-grade games there. In two of those years I won best defensive first-grade player awards.

Ken 'Killer' Kearney was the coach at the club. He had been the captain of St George and was a rugby league and rugby union international. He had been involved with the St George club when they had that big run of Premiership wins in the late '50s early '60s. Strangely enough, in either the first or second season I was there, the club brought in a selector who was a little bit radical. People could not understand what he was talking about; he only lasted three-quarters of the season. He had arguments with people about his selections and the people he wanted to play. His name happened to be Jack Gibson!

Killer, though, had a reputation as a good coach. He was tough, one of the old-school tough guys. In those days it was the survival of the fittest. At the time if you looked at the South Sydney side, they had the likes of John O'Neil, George Piggins, Elwin Walters, Gary Stevens, Ron Coote, Bob McCarthy, John Morgan and John Sattler. They were all tough and skilful players! That was what it was about in those days.

I have actually been knocked out on a few kick-offs! Just watching the ball go down the field and jogging back to where it was. I then had to pick myself up and wonder who hit me on the way past! You could not compare the game we played to the game played and coached now; you had to be aggressive to survive.

It must be said that, strange as it may seem for someone of such a relatively small stature, Monie was no stranger to aggression.

Equally strange is believing this aggressive streak actually exists, given his persona. Monie is a man who rarely loses his temper or control. He always seems cool, calm and collected and in control, a far cry from the aggressive, bristling little stand-off he obviously was:

> I have always been aggressive, even when we lived in Scone. My mother tells a good story about when the rodeos used to come to town. I used to go down when I was about twelve years old to the showground where the rodeo was set up. I would fight in those boxing tents, you know the sort of thing where a guy would bang a drum and call on anyone in the crowd to fight this guy or that guy. People used to throw money into the ring when I was fighting, which I got to keep. I used to bring money home to Mom every time the rodeo hit town. I continued to fight in the tents at the shows into my early twenties. When we moved down to Ocean Beach, three nights a week I would get the bus to Woy-Woy and go to the back of the hotel there. There was an old guy who taught boxing; we used to fight in an old tin shed at the back of the Woy-Woy Hotel. From a very early age I did not mind physical confrontation.
>
> I had a season with Tommy Bishop at Cronulla, my last season there. We got into a bit of trouble, or perhaps I should say we started a bit of trouble. We always left it up to the front row to finish it. We had Noel Gallagher, Dave Cooper, Monty Porter, who had been in the St George side with Ken Kearney, Paul Taylor, Alan McRichie, a good loose forward called Graham Sanms, and we had Warren Ryan in the centre who went on to coach successfully, so there were plenty of people around to finish what Tommy and I kicked off. Before Tommy Bishop arrived, the half-back was a guy called Terry Hughes and he won the first ever Rothman's medal for the player of the year. So we were a

real good side.

I actually held the record for most tries in match. I got four [tries] one game against Newtown. It stood until Ettinshausen broke it early in his career. I think he got five, but I held the record for a long while.

Looking back, it seems strange that the young John Monie, who appeared to have the rugby world at his feet, turned his back on it. At the tender age of twenty-three he left Cronulla to return to Woy-Woy, the Central Coast and his surfboard:

The problem was I was homesick. I missed the coast and my friends, the good surf which was up there. I just decided I had given it a go in Sydney, and I was keen to get back into the surf a little bit more. I had an offer to go back as captain-coach at Woy-Woy, which meant I could earn some money but still have the summer time to go surfing as well. Two of the three seasons I was at Cronulla I spent my money on a plane fare to Hawaii, spending two or three months out there surfing. If you surfed in those days, the late '60s early '70s, Hawaii was the big challenge. Once I was flush with a couple of thousand dollars from playing; that is where I went to spend it!

Even though he was very young to be coaching the game, he had no doubts about his ability to be successful. After all, he had played the game for seventeen years, three of them at the very highest level and three at the highest country level. Perhaps it was the fact that he was coaching so young that made him one of the best coaches the game has seen.

If you played half or five-eight in those days it meant you had a knowledge of the game. It went with the position. You understood what had to be done, you were in a thinking position. Even when I was playing at under-seventeen level, I was always good at getting other players to play around me, and directing players and, importantly, leading from the front. If someone needed to be hit, then that's what had to be done. I played until I was thirty-three and I broke my arm. I also had knee problems. I was playing on, like a lot of those captain-coaches in New South Wales. Guys who could not run very much any more: they steered teams around the park and did the thinking. They did what had to be done.

In the middle of all that I had a spell up in Newcastle. I went up there to the toughest rugby league outside Sydney, in fact it was possibly even tougher than in the days I played up there. It was a comp which saw just Newcastle sides playing against each other. Dennis Ward was the captain-coach up in Newcastle. He had just finished as the Australian half-back. He went to a very rich club up there in Wests that had a reputation for buying good players, so they were very much disliked in the Newcastle competition, which was all steel mills and dockyards. They still have a reputation up there as being the area which beat the English touring side more than any other, when they came to Australia in those days. That was through the '70s.

Talk about tough and aggressive – Newcastle wrote the book on that. I enjoyed the time up in Newcastle, I had very good times. But toward the end of my time up there, Dennis Ward, who had heaps of experience as an Australian representative, asked if I could talk to the players. He felt he was not getting through to them and asked if I would talk on his behalf. So even up there I was coaching and acting as a go-between, between him and the players.

Communicating with players has come easy to me; it is something I have always been able to do. People think it is not an easy skill; my feeling is that people who talk from the heart and talk a simple language, that's the right way to put it I think, will always be successful. Most rugby league players will not identify with the school-teacher type of approach. When it gets right down to the nitty-gritty, they need somebody they can look in the eye and know that it's coming from the right place. Part of it, also, is the belief players have that you as a coach have a sound knowledge of the game, and the fundamentals of the game. Also that what you are saying will get them out of tough situations, will win them games.

When I decided to stop playing, again, I was lucky because Woy-Woy said they wanted me to coach them for as long as I wanted. I must confess that I did not find it much different not being on the field. I felt a lot easier on Mondays! It was, though, still the same, planning training sessions. Also I knew by that stage I already had a team of people that worked for me and I have always stuck with them, been loyal to them. I have always had good relationships with people who have worked for me, and we have hung in there for a long time.

Monie's nickname down under is the 'Iceman' (from the book *Coaches Who Shaped the Game 80–90*), mainly due to the cool, calm, detached demeanour which always appears to surface on match days. It is not something he would necessarily agree with or even subscribe to. He prefers to look on it as being focused. It is a focus born out of necessity. As he says:

If you want to be successful you have to be one step ahead of everybody else. If you needed to be one step ahead to win, then that was what I was prepared to do. I was prepared to do whatever I had to do within the rules to win a game. I was, and still am, always into the game, very focused and trying to stay ahead of what the players were doing at the time. So that when the time came for them to do something different, I had already got it planned what we were going to do. If someone got injured, I knew who I was going to put where. I have always been able to watch a game and stay one step ahead of what everyone else was doing.

Perhaps one of the reasons Monie has been successful is the loyalty he has always shown to his staff and the loyalty given in return. He believes that you have to build on success, which always takes time. Time for the players to get to know what he wanted of them. Time for his own staff to learn what was expected of them. He has always stayed at clubs a long time and so has been successful. Even at Woy-Woy he was there as captain-coach eight seasons, during which time they won six championships. As he put it, 'We were always on the money!' There are some coaches, as there are players, who have had more clubs than a top golfer, but Monie is not one of them. The loyalty factor is important to him; it helps him do the job.

I have been at the top level now for twenty seasons and I have only coached at Parramatta, Wigan, Auckland and now London. I value loyalty, I value that virtue in people, and in my players. Peter Louis, my playing partner at Woy-Woy, was my reserve-grade coach at Woy-Woy, then he was reserve-grade coach at Parramatta for me. I recommended he get the job at Parramatta when I left and they did not give it to him. As a result he went to North Sydney and won a coach of the year award while he was there.

Bob Lanigan was my conditioner at Woy-Woy right through the '70s, then I got him a job at Parramatta. He also came to Wigan with me and also down to Auckland. When I got to Wigan I inherited Bill Hartley and I still keep in touch with him. Dean Bell played for me at Wigan, and captained the side for me. He came to Auckland for me as well. Andy Goodway, who had played for me at Wigan, was my reserve-grade coach at Wigan when I went back there.

So there is a familiar line through everything I have done, that is being loyal to a club, loyal to players and loyal to people who have worked for me. When you have a team you can rely on, you just know jobs are going to get done. More importantly, they get done in a way you would want them to be done. Also they understand my humour, my sarcasm, whatever it is about me.

It was in 1980 that Monie severed his connection with the Woy-Woy club, when he moved into the Sydney competition. It brought about a reunion with that very same radical selector who had managed in a short time to upset most of the Cronulla hierarchy: Jack Gibson.

What happened was Jack rang up and told me that through his scouting people, who watched a great deal of rugby league, it had been brought to his attention how successful we had been at Woy-Woy. More importantly, perhaps, was the fact that we had been successful with teams which possibly should not have won the competition. He also remembered me from his first 'short' stint at Cronulla and how well I had done there. He told me he was taking over at Parramatta in 1981 and he was going to change things around at the club. He took guys off the front gate and put them on the changing-room doors, masseurs suddenly found themselves kit men. When he took over he was taking in all of his own staff, and it was something which had not been done a lot in Sydney, at that time. It is now common practice. I can remember what Jack actually said to me when he phoned: 'I am not offering security, I'm offering opportunity.' He also told me that people should go where they'll be happy, and that's important in coaching; I never forgot that.

The club had never won a first-grade competition, although they had won a heap of lower-grade comps. They could not get over the line in the first grade, therefore they had a lot of good players at the club but some were coming to the end of their careers. Because they had so many, the second-grade side was nearly always as good as the first-grade side. Jack cleared out a lot of players because he always had a clear idea of what he wanted to do. So everyone went – coaches, players and other staff – that Jack did not want. He offered me the job as skills coach and as coach of the second-grade team.

At the time, while working at Woy-Woy, I was also working at Gosford at the Central Coast youth club, where I took fitness classes, gymnastic classes and trampolining and that sort of stuff. My boss there was a guy who was the Australian trampolining coach at the time. He was one of the first to use video tape, or 'cine' I suppose, the old reel to reel stuff. That also helped me with my coaching because he was really into coaching as well. I had a wonderful job, where I could go there to coach a couple of schools twice a week, but there was plenty of time to sit and talk to him about coaching at the top level. He was really spot on at the time, using cameras with his trampolining team and would play it back on the reel to reel. He could then analyse mistakes and work out how to correct faults in his athletes. It was a very enjoyable time for me, coachingwise, because I was able to grow as a coach by benefiting from ideas from another sport. That fella's name was Fred Austine!

It was Monie's first encounter with the technology which appears to have swamped the game of rugby league in the 1990s. Now it seems the game is about statistics and video recordings. Even in those very early days, Monie realised the importance of technology. He never lost sight of what it actually was, namely a tool for the coaches to use: 'Most of the best stuff in coaching comes from the gut or from the heart. You have to use whatever means available to you. I use statistics as much as any other coach; we analyse the game and break it down, but at the end of the day video and statistics are certainly not my master.'

When he arrived at Parramatta it was the Jack Gibson show, or, perhaps to be more accurate, the Jack Gibson–Ron Massey show. Monie was there simply as a skills and reserve-grade coach. He was part of a team, most of whom were in awe of Gibson. Monie, though not in awe, had tremendous respect and regard for the coach:

> Jack was just fantastic, he was the source of everyone's light, he was that far ahead of the game at the time, and in a different way. It is hard to put into words just what he had; he was a unique character. From a club which had never won a first-grade competition, Jack won the comp in 1981, 1982 and 1983. That was just unheard of stuff, for someone to come in and do that to a club!
>
> Working with Jack altered me as a coach. I think everyone who came in contact with him was in awe of him. Jack quickly recognised that I was not in awe of him and I think that is why we got on together so well. Everyone used to be intimidated when they were around Jack, but I treated him the way I treated everybody. He was someone I admired and I was in awe of the way he approached the job but I was not intimidated by him as much as everyone else seemed to be.
>
> He did have an odd way with words, and a lot of the time players and coaches did not understand what he was talking about, me included. He did, though, have a great go-between at the club with Ronnie Massey. He used to help Jack with the videos. He would write out all the stuff for Jack to use at team meetings. He was the facts and figures guy. He could tell you technically everything that was going on, ball control and all of that; he was the first to use that terminology then. Massey had it all at his

fingertips. Massey supplied all of that. Jack, though, got you to play good! It was a really unusual working combination that the two of them had.

Massey was very cutting and very sarcastic . . . abrupt. He could be very brusque and to the point with players, whereas Jack was laid back, cool, but he could numb a player with his stare; he would not have to say anything. As soon as Jack looked at you, you knew if you were in trouble or not. Jack did not have to say a lot, and when he said anything that was the end of it. A lot of the time Jack never let it come to that, he let Massey handle that side of things. Massey would even read a lot of Jack's comments on the game at the team meetings. They would go through each player and if Jack could not think of something then Massey would say, 'You remember at that play, when we said this or that happened.' Jack would then take it over from there. It was a wonderful little combination they had.

There are a million Jack Gibson stories. I think everybody has one, but the one that sums everything up was the incident I had with Stephen Sharp. Sharp was a good tough-tackling, second-row forward. Jack had trained him with the first-grade side all week because he wanted to use him in the first team. In those days you had to finish the second-grade game so that you could be a replacement for the first-grade side.

I did not have Steve Sharp all week; Jack had him, and had a plan for him in first grade. In the second-grade game that weekend I had a couple of very good attacking players sitting on the bench for me. In the last ten minutes of the game we were behind, I think, by around two points. Jack and Ron Massey had already gone into the sheds with the first-grade side. I sent a message out to bring Steve Sharp off and to put Neil Hunt and another guy on! I thought they could win the game for us. I saw Steve shake his head knowing that he could not come off because he was fully aware of the rule and also that Jack had run him all week and was going to use him in first grade. If I brought him off in the last five minutes he could not play. The rule was that a player had to finish the reserve-grade match still on the paddock, otherwise he could not be on the subs bench for the reserve grade.

I sent the message out again to get him off and get the attacking players on. Just before the hooter went we scored a try, and I, also just before we scored, saw Massey coming back out of the sheds walking toward me. You could see the steam coming out of his ears. The crowd was going crazy as well, as if they knew what I had done. Just as he got to me we had scored in the corner and we won the game. Massey said to me, 'You better get into the changing-room; Jack wants to see you.'

It was one of those situations where you walk into the changing-room and there is a bit of noise. All of a sudden it went dead quiet; everybody who was in that room was looking at me. Jack was talking to someone, then turned around and saw me. Ron Massey had given me an earful all the way in and Jack said: 'You knew I had Sharp with me all week, that he was part of the plans for the first grade this week.'

I told him, yeah.

'Well, what were you thinking of?'

'Well, I was just trying to win the game, Jack.'

You could have heard a pin drop in that changing-room; it was unbelievable. Jack just sort of looked at me and smiled and said, 'What was the score?'

I told him we won it on the bell and he just said, 'Well, that's what I pay you for, Monie.'

He turned around and just gave his team talk. That sort of sums him up in a way. Mind you, I had ruined his first-grade plans, though.

The reason that situation happened comes back to what

> I was saying earlier about having that focus on the game. My thoughts were how am I going to win this? What do I have to do? It was a tight game – how can I pull it out? I have been good at winning tight games when you look back over my career. That is because of the focus. I knew Jack wanted Sharp but I knew I could not win the game, and at that moment of trying to win the game it never came into my mind that Jack needed Sharp for first grade, it was gone. All that mattered was winning the game. I looked through the players on the bench, looked at the players on the field and said, 'I know how I can win this game.' I need to bring off defensive players and put on attacking ones! Bang, I did it, and the way Jack accepted that probably summed the both of us up.

Gibson must have been impressed with Monie's single-mindedness: he did not sack him. On the contrary, when he shocked the game by quitting the Parramatta club it was Monie whom he recommended should replace him as head coach. That was a little way into the future, but not that far off. Soon, it was to be Monie who was making plans for players in first grade, Monie who was to take over the reins from the man considered to be the guru of modern coaching of rugby league football. Like everything he had ever done, John Monie simply took it in his stride; he knew what had to be done and focused on the job of being head coach at the Parramatta club. It did, though, prove not as easy as it had first appeared.

3

THE PARRAMATTA HEAD COACH

'The best coaches are those who understand their players and have a simple playing system the players understand.'

It is a brave man, indeed, who resigns on the back of three straight successful years with a rugby league club. That, though, was just what Jack Gibson did at Parramatta. To say the world of Australian rugby league was shocked would be an understatement! In truth, those 'in the know' with Gibson saw it coming because it was something he had done before. He was a man who preferred to leave a club while it was in good shape, rather than flog the players to their last ounce of effort and then leave.

Monie witnessed the departure first hand, but he is the first to admit he did not appreciate the pressure a successful head coach like Gibson was under. It was this kind of pressure that was to cost Monie dearly in his first season as head coach.

> I think what happened with Jack was that after his three seasons at the club, and don't forget prior to him coming the club had never won the competition at first grade, he had done enough. He brought in new staff, got rid of older

players and won the competition in 1981, 1982 and 1983. What else was there for him to achieve? The pressure in coaching is pretty intense. If you take the intensity on a coach in England you would need to multiply that intensity by a couple to get some idea of the pressure a coach in Australia would be under! Certainly after three seasons at the club when he had won three competitions in a row, I felt that Jack was beginning to get worn down, either by his own expectation, or by the expectations of others as a result of those wins, to keep the team winning. As it turned out, I started to go through the same pressures at Wigan in 1991, 1992 and 1993, when they won everything.

The more you win, the more people expect you to win, and the more style they expect from your teams. They do not want you to grind out wins, certainly after the supporters think they are on a good thing.

So I know how he felt after those three seasons. It was starting to get to him a little. He felt the time was right to step back from it all. Jack felt the time was right, but I did not really see it coming because back at that time I didn't recognise the signs! I was young, full of enthusiasm and just breaking into the game at that top level. I was full of beans, I did not have the responsibility of the club on my shoulders. I had to coach skills and look after reserve grade, with some input regarding tactics and certain pieces of set play which we would use in games. I did not understand the pressures of the head coaching job.

It was big news when Jack left the club, because he was held in such high regard by everybody. He had done as before at Eastern Suburbs and just finished with the club. He had sides afterwards which were just verging on greatness, when he would say, 'Well, that's enough, mate,' and leave. He certainly did not wring everything out of a side and then go, but deliberately went with sides on an upward curve! He left sides in pretty good shape. That is something I have always tried to follow; when you leave a club they should be stronger than when you arrive. Jack left the place in pretty good shape.

The esteem in which Monie held Gibson is obvious, and this was matched by almost everyone in the Aussie game. But Gibson did not regard himself so highly that he in turn could not regard others in the game with respect. It was obvious from his actions when leaving the Parramatta club that he appreciated his reserve-grade coach. Monie explained just how he got the hot seat Gibson had left:

> I think Jack walked into the board of directors and said, 'I have had three seasons, turned the club around, won this, and done that for you. I do not think you have to go anywhere looking for a coach. You have got your next first-grade coach working with the reserve grade here. Don't advertise for a coach, don't do anything, the coach is here, the players want him. I am confident he can do the job for you and win you another competition. I am finished!'
>
> Whether the board had a meeting after that I have no idea, but Dennis Fitzgerald, who was in charge of the board, called me in and I was hired. That first season in 1984 was certainly a shock to me and by the end of it I really understood what being tired mentally was all about; I knew how Jack must have felt. When you step from the shadows and suddenly you are there up front, it is very, very tiring.
>
> The major changes were simply the extra responsibility, also the expectations placed on me. At the time I wasn't able to recognise that because I was so full of it. I wanted to do the job; I was so keen and enthusiastic. Everything was in front of me and I had a very good football team. Winning a grand final in Australia is just the hardest

challenge any of you are going to face in rugby league. I think, though, I was bordering on being naive as far as expectations, pressure, and everything else to do with being a head coach goes. I just jumped in, boots and all, I was so keen to do the job.

One thing that did help was that I had no need to win the players over; they were happy that I had simply stepped up a grade. The club did not miss a beat, although it was still a tough competition and a tight one. The nucleus of players who had been there the season before was still in place and would remain for my first season as head coach. In terms of the playing strength, Jack had left the club in pretty good shape. The other thing was that the players still had a couple more seasons in them. History shows that. We lost in one of the lowest-scoring grand finals, ever, in 1984, by 6–4 with Mick Cronin scoring the try for us. We made the play-off again in 1985 and were eliminated 7–6 in the final, and in the 1986 season we won the lot! The pre-season, we were the club champions, had two sides in grand finals, we won the mid-week cup and we won the grand final. That 1986 grand final was the lowest scoring ever; we took it 4–2. Again Cronin scored all our points, this time with two goals. I remember that we'd had a very good win in the Major Semi by 28–6, prior to the grand final against Canterbury, and then again in the grand final it went down to one of those real tight games.

One of the major pressures, when I look back on that 1984 season, was the expectations of the Parramatta blue and gold army. I have often thought that had it not been my first season as a first-grade coach, we might well have won a title! You always look back and hope you have improved as a coach. I just felt that the grind towards the end of the season took its toll. I have never, since 1984, felt like I was being worn down, as I was that first season. It was a mental thing, something you could not quite put your finger on. Looking back now, I can say that mentally I was starting to get tired.

One of the things which has been with Monie throughout his career, both as a player and as a coach, is his desire always to strive to get an edge over his opponents. He was among the first to use a dietician at the club. He also brought in a sports psychologist from the city university and gave him sessions with the players. This was at a time when sports psychology generally was in its infancy, certainly as far as rugby league was concerned.

I brought the psychologist in because at that time my experience told me that there was a role for sports psychologists to play. I felt it was in the mental approach to the game, to the goal setting, writing things down, putting things in order, as it were. As a rugby league coach, I was concerned with things like playing the balls, set pieces and defensive lines and moving up, whereas I came to the conclusion then that the role of the sports psychologist was in actually setting down a pattern for players to work towards in how to help each other. How to go about structuring personal goals, team goals and such like, really how to put that side of things all together. In those early days the psychologists were saying they wanted to talk to players; one wanted to talk to the players at half-time! That was the last thing I wanted. Now, looking back on it, I think I did the right thing; I did not want them anywhere near the guys at half-time. I did not want a player coming in at half-time thinking he had to sit down and 'express his anxieties to a sports psychologist'.

The players are like me – they are always looking for an edge, something which is going to make just a little bit of difference. If you get right down to the nitty-gritty, some

> weeks you only win by a point. It's half a step, or has the sprint work really worked? I have always believed if you have not got speed you have not got it, but a sprint coach and a techniques coach might just be able to get that little bit extra out of you. I have always favoured specialised coaching, and although I have not used them regularly, I have been in favour of sports psychologists if they could give my team an edge.

He also followed the lead set by Jack Gibson in studying the training methods used by American football teams and the weight-training programmes they used. He was a regular visitor to the States in his early years as head coach.

The other thing he prided himself on was being well read, and this still applies today. It matters not to him what sport it is, for he has always felt you can learn from other coaches and players. He would look at anything that he felt would make him be a better coach or help him to improve his players. He talked to the coaches and players of the Aussie rules game down in Melbourne, to basketball and American football teams. The discipline did not matter to Monie. What was important was anything they could offer him.

When he arrived at Parramatta, he found Jack Gibson and Ron Massey were already great exponents of the use of game videos. Massey in particular, in the early 1980s was, in Monie's opinion, 'right on the money'. He could look at a video and tell which players were not giving 100 per cent or which players were resting on the short side of the field. Video analysis was most certainly one of Ron Massey's areas of expertise. In team meetings it was Ron Massey who would remind Gibson of the details gleaned from the match video, pinpointing areas which Gibson would then take up with individual players.

The other great quality Monie has always had is patience. He has never rushed into a club and immediately started to change things around. His philosophy, unlike some other coaches, is simply, 'If it is not broken, don't try to mend it.' To be fair, though, at Parramatta there was simply no need for change.

> We did not change much because a lot of the stuff we did in the first-grade side had been tried in our reserve-grade side. If Jack had liked it, he just moved it on to first grade. That was one of the good things about Jack. When he saw something that he liked he would call me in and ask, 'What was that you did last week when you were trying to win the game?' I would give him a brief on what we had done. Often he would say 'I like that,' so he would take it and it would become part of the first-grade game plan. That was one of the reasons that I got the job at Parramatta, because Jack recognised people who could add something to the organisation. He was always prepared to use people's ideas, and this is something I have tried to take on when I have employed lower-grade coaches at the clubs I have been with. It did not matter to me if they were conditioners or coaches, if they came up with a good idea then everyone at the club was a winner. It is a philosophy I have always had; I think Jack also had it.

When Monie took over at Parramatta, all the great players from that glorious three-year period under Gibson were still at the club.

> If you start at the backs, Paul Taylor, Eric Grothe, Hunt was on one wing, Graham Atkins on the other wing. Steve Ella, Michael Cronin were in the centres; Brett Kenny and Peter Stirling were the halves, they were all just household names. Geoff Bugden, Mares, Stan Jurd, Leabeater, Steven Edge (Bob O'Reilly had just retired), Peter Wynn, John Muggleston, who is working with the Wallabies at the moment, and Ray Price was there as well.

> There was a great front-rower there by the name of Paul Mares, whom I picked up when we were trialling about two hundred and fifty players for three spots at the club. Then we used to grade out fifty-five players at the club. I was out on one of the back paddocks, looking at one of the games with all these hopefuls. There was a big kid out there who was great, who started off in those trials and went right through. I reported back to Jack that I thought I had found us a front-rower. He went on to be one of the really good Parramatta front-row players. Unfortunately he was plagued with injury, which eventually finished him, but we were a little bit shocked when we came to grade him and found out he was only sixteen! But he was a monster. So we had a lot of good players.
>
> They started in 1980 and went right through to 1986 and nobody defected. There were a lot of clubs pulling and trying to pinch the players but the bond was so good they resisted all the temptations to change clubs. We just didn't lose any players and it was a great six years.

That loyalty between coach and player which was present between Gibson and his players was also there with Monie. During his time at Parramatta, and also at Wigan and Auckland, there were only a handful of players who left those clubs because they felt they were being unfairly treated. Monie is the first to admit that he likes to stick with his players. He is well aware of the efforts and the sacrifices they make for him to play first grade. When he sees them bust themselves in that way he feels he should be loyal at the other end of it. As he says:

> When players give all you ask of them and then some more; when they give that bit above and beyond the call of duty, they have earned your loyalty. In many ways they have a right to demand that loyalty from their coach. I was pleased with the way I handled players; I feel it was one of

my strong qualities. Unfortunately, I was so successful at it, the news never got out, people never saw it, particularly in New Zealand.

I refuse to admit that the Auckland years were a failure. We finished mid-table in our first two seasons. The people over there were not patient enough; they were not prepared to wait. We had a plan and were developing junior Kiwi players, young New Zealand talent, and they weren't prepared to wait for it coming through. We didn't want the Kiwi talent scattered all over Australia and New Zealand.

Coaching is not just about first grade; it is an on-going development, and coaches have to be aware of that. Also, administrators have to be aware of that, too, but many of them, particularly chairmen over in England, simply don't understand that. It was a point I stressed when I went back to Wigan in 1998. Regardless of all the good development work the club is doing, if, out of your under-19 team, you only get two or three players who go on to become first-grade players, that is a good return. If you are lucky, every few years you may well unearth one outstanding talent. People tend to look at development programmes and think because they are developing a great under-19, team they are going to get eight or nine players who are going to play first grade. That is not going to happen at places like Auckland or Wigan. It is a real misconception, and the junior development people are probably most at fault here. They think a lot are going to come through. Take it from me, you do not get a lot coming through, even from outstanding under-19 sides. Pat yourself on the back if you get two or three!

The last Wigan board I worked with did not understand that. When I told them, they sat around the table in shock and told me how much money they had spent on development work. They could not understand that if I was lucky I would get four players from all their hard work and cash.

While at Wigan in his first spell, players like Andy Farrell, Jason Robinson, B-J Mather and Mick Cassidy made it through to first grade. He had similar success at Parramatta; sadly, he was not to remain at Auckland long enough to see the development plans come to fruition. However, building championship teams in itself creates other problems. Championship sides do not change their personnel a great deal, which stifles opportunities for junior players to come through. You may well move one player in and one out at the end of a season; one or two may go, and then it is simply a matter of keeping the standard up with the replacement players. It is a tricky matter to maintain this balance, but Monie has never been afraid to give youngsters a chance, even in his championship sides.

> Young players, be they English or Australian, are always pleased to come into sides like that. They know they only have to do what you have put them in the team to do; they don't have to win the game for you. They come in and hold up their end of the bargain. I have had young players who were scared senseless before a game. I have made them stand up in front of the other players and say, 'The coach has brought me into this team. He expects me to do this and this and this, and I will not let you down.' Then I have got the senior players to say, 'If you can do that for us, we will not let you down.' That takes a lot of pressure off a youngster coming into a good side. Lee Gilmour was outstanding when I brought him into the Wigan side in 1998, using that approach. You must remember it is harder to stay at the top than it is to get to the top! It is difficult when you have to perform at the top level, week in week out, year after year. That is the true test of any man or any good player.

One of the difficult tasks a coach faces is telling an older player that he has had his day and it is time to move on. Monie, given the loyalty he had for players who had given him their all, felt the anguish more than most. He certainly felt it at Parramatta.

> Pricey and Mick Cronin were two of the best examples of that. They both knew it. Cronin should have retired when Mark Laurie poked him in the eye, leaving him with a scratched eyeball and detached retina. Even when I played him in the grand final Cronin's vision was not good on one side. It was just my stubbornness as a coach and his as a player not to retire, not to let him finish that way. I kept telling him, 'I am going to put you back in first grade!' I also told him, 'You are going to be the goal-kicker in the grand final.' I refused to let him retire! One of the reasons I did this was due to the sight I had of 'The Crow' at the opening of the new stadium.
>
> As we opened up the new stadium at Parramatta, a sad sight and one of the saddest memories I have got of Parramatta was Cronin standing in the tunnel when the team was ready for battle. 'Pricey' was always greasy all over his face and was leading the team out. Everything was as it normally was, except Cronin, who was standing there in his Parramatta coat and tie in the tunnel with his head down. It was a big day, the opening of the stadium and Mick was not out there playing! That was why I wanted him to play on and make the grand final team! (If we made it.)
>
> In the grand final he nearly missed the ball for the first goal-kick he took; he just could not see – the poor bugger! He had to be part of that grand final, though. When we won it, Pricey was thirty-three and Cronin was thirty-five. They knew the end had come and it was time to retire. That was really their grand final. I had tasted it as second-grade coach in 1981, 1982 and 1983; when Jack Gibson won the first grade in 1984 I had missed it narrowly. Pricey always

said that the 1986 grand final was for John Monie, but I think it will always be remembered for Pricey and 'The Crow', and I am happy for it to be remembered as such. It was a fantastic time, full of emotion, and that is what the game is all about.

The two front-rowers we had, the 'Bookends'; they became legends that year: Bugden and Leabeater. They were just fantastic characters. I had them on a fining system to lose weight. One of the sponsors said, 'What weight do you want them at?' I think I wanted them both under 116 kg, and neither of them could reach that! Then it made the papers and we would have photographers down at training. In grand final week the headline was 'They Made It' as they had got under 116 kg. They weighed in on Tuesday and there was a photo of them smashing the scales up with huge sledgehammers! Neither of them ever got under 116 kg – they lied! They used to starve on the day of the weigh-in and do all kinds of things to cheat the scales.

They once said to me they were thinking about me and the club dietician one Sunday. The dietician made all the players keep a record of how many drinks they had. I think it was Bugden who said he had drunk thirty-two Jack Daniels and Coke! And he told me, 'After the tenth one I was thinking about you, coach, because I switched to Jack Daniels and Diet Coke!' With those two and Pricey and the Crow retiring, it was a great time.

During his time at Parramatta, Monie experienced the highs and lows of the game. He coached a losing side in a grand final and then two years later coached a side which won.

I think we lost the first grand final because of fatigue! Also Canterbury were a very good, tough, well-coached side. It was my first season in first grade, and I think I had been

> worn down throughout the season. Now I am good at not feeling the pressure and being relaxed in those situations, but that first year was tough on me. Not tough on me at the time, I am not saying I felt it at the time, but, when I look back, 'Jeez'. I have always been able to come up with good things and good plays in tight situations. I just remember looking back at the loss: it was 6–4.

Whilst he was willing to take the blame for the final defeat, in Monie's defence it must be pointed out that there were two factors in that final over which he had no control. Both probably contributed to the defeat. The first was an injury to centre Steve Ella, who was a potent strike force for the Eels. He was forced out of the game after only seven minutes. Then, with the Eels leading 4–0, thanks to a try by 'The Crow', Ray Price was injured making a tackle. Before he could recover and get back into the defensive line, the 'Bulldogs' ran from dummy half and caught the Eels' defence napping. The rest, as they say, is history. Canterbury won the game 6–4. However, Monie felt that the Canterbury side were a powerful outfit and any game against them was always going to be close, as the grand final showed.

> There were great battles going on between Parramatta and Canterbury at that time. They were the 'dogs of war'; they were the tough side; they would kill you as soon as look at you. They were a very tough side when you looked through the team they had: Peter Kelly, Peter Tunks, Mark Bugden, Langmack and Gillespie. They would just give it to you, so they were really hard battles. The Mortimer brothers were there, and the Hughes. All in all they were a very good side. There was always this real 'thing' going on between the two clubs. One of my best wins was in a round game against them when we had about six of our under-21 team in first grade, and we beat them. We were ground-sharing with them at the time around 1985. Parramatta stadium was

being built, so we played there when they were away.

People often ask me how you raise a team after a grand final defeat. It is not so difficult – simply because it is all over. Grand finals are about black and white; you either win or you lose – there is nothing in between. It is a year's work. To get there is a great achievement, but after I lost that first grand final I thought, 'I would rather not be in a grand final than lose it.' In 1998, when I went to Wembley with Wigan and lost when we were overwhelming favourites to win, I did not have that same feeling of 'I would rather not be here than lose.' I think I was mature enough to say it was a great experience and we can turn this great Wigan club around. Back in '84 I thought I would rather not be at a grand final. Forget the occasion, forget the build-up through the week, forget the police escort from Parramatta: I would rather not be in it. That was my immediate feeling at the loss.

I have always felt part of the wins and the losses my teams have been involved in, so I contributed to that defeat. I always take a back step with the wins because I feel it is the players who should get all the credit, although you certainly feel part of it. I think, however, that I should be the one who steps forward when we lose a game. I have always tried to represent the team when we have lost. When we have won I feel as happy as the players but tend to melt into the background.

Winning the final in '86, it did not matter to me that it was the lowest-scoring final. We won by the same margin we lost the '84 final. We had good wins against the other finals club in the build-up to the final. In the major semi we went straight through to the final, beating them by around 30 points, and played some outstanding rugby league. The grand final, though, is not about good rugby; it is, as I said, black or white. You win or you lose. It's good for your heart if you win by 20 or 30 points but it doesn't matter how many you win by as long as you win. I have never been one to go back and say, 'Gee, we can learn a lot of good lessons out of that loss.' What a loss does is make you work harder on the training paddock and pay more attention to detail. When you are winning all the time you start to slip up with the small things in the game because you feel good and are rolling along. You have that confidence and feeling that if you keep going you will win. Losing makes you pay more attention to the little things in the game.

We took mistake-free football as far as we could in that final. By that I mean, if there was a chance a pass would be knocked down, then don't throw it! That was the game in Australia then. It was developing along those American football lines. If it was possible to pass a ball and your teammate was 100 per cent sure of catching it, then you passed. It was about mistake-free football and about field position, and it was about having good players who could play under that sort of pressure. That system bred really mentally tough players who refused to do the wrong thing.

Now, ten or fifteen years on, we have gone full circle. Coaches are saying to players you have got to express yourself, you have got to take some chances, you have got to get the pass out. Now I coach off-loads, I coach second-phase plays, I encourage players I coach not to be uptight, not to tuck the ball away. Now I continually stress to players about using their feet, trying to beat the guy, getting the ball free, getting it flopped back. I think we had taken that form of error-free football just about as far as we could by the '86 grand final. The scores in those grand finals reflected that. The 1984 final was 6–4, the 1985 final 7–6 and the 1986 final 4–2.

When the hooter went in the '86 final, the only feeling that came over me was one of relief! I just felt everything go. You often read about the weight being taken off someone's shoulders, well, that actually happened to me; I felt light. In 1999 Shaun Edwards' dad showed me the tape of that '86 grand final. It was good to watch it because I had not seen it in a very long time. I saw the relief, even on the tape. As I said, once I got to the dressing sheds it turned into Pricey and Crow's day. I was happy to fade into the background.

I stayed for another three seasons after that grand final win. The nucleus of that very good side had come to the end. We had lost Pricey and replaced him with Bob Lindner, who did not work out. He played pretty well but he did not fit into Parramatta. We tried to replace those good players but the chemistry of that good side was broken and the time had come for someone new who could say, 'Okay, we've got as much out of that era as we can; let's start again.'

Monie's Parramatta days were at an end, but the rest he was looking for was not to be – thanks to the silver tongue of an English club chairman.

I don't think I can look at my time at Parramatta and say there was one game or one period which stood out above the rest. I enjoyed my time there. From '81 to '83 as reserve-grade coach, through '84 to '87, even up to the time I left, they were just wonderful, wonderful memories. People like Bob O'Reilly and Kevin Stephens were always fun to be around, and Stephen Edge, who is still there to this day. Fantastic characters – there were just a lot of good people in the place at once.

Eric Grothe was probably the most explosive runner of the football in the world at the time; in training, though, he was just a big laid-back character who would only run as far as he had to. When we trained he would sit out on the side line in the semi-darkness hiding; occasionally I would call over and ask him if everything was okay with him. He was fun to be around because come Sunday he did the job. As I said, he would not run further than was needed. Once he crossed the try-line, that was where he put the ball down. If the in-goal area was ten metres, he would make sure he put the ball down on the line. In truth, you did not need an in-goal area for Eric!

In pre-season we used to have time trials and the players would run around the streets of Parramatta and Mount Pritchard. The players would be out on the road from around an hour and a half to two hours or so, and this was at the height of the summer. Anyone who came in after the cut-off time would not be in good books with anybody on the coaching staff. It was a real test because it used to get real hot out there. Whenever we had one of the time trials Eric Grothe used to come in maybe thirty or forty minutes after everyone had finished. One day we were sitting around waiting for him to finish; most of the players had showered when he arrived. As he came in we could see there was a bit of dampness on his shirt, which was most unusual for Eric: he rarely broke sweat on one of these runs. When we asked him about it, he told us that a lady had recognised him when he was a little way from home and had hosed him down!

Eventually I had to stop the runs because we had a youngster, Adrian Sligar, who had been holidaying in Europe and only returned to the Aussie summer two days before one of those horrendous runs. When he finished, he collapsed with heat exhaustion; we needed the paramedics to bring him round. He was okay a couple of days later, but it scared the hell out of me at the time, and prompted my decision to put a stop to the road runs.

Brett Kenny was also laid back, but he had a burning desire to be successful; he would only do what he had to in training. He would, though, do plenty of work away from the place and not tell a lot of people about it. He used to dislike doing his weight training and he would not do it very well at the club. When a couple of the players retired and they went round to Brett's place one day, they found he had a fantastic gym in his garage. He was one of those closet trainers who would do whatever he had to, to be successful. I would watch the reserve grade play for the first forty minutes and go into the sheds after fifteen or twenty minutes of the second half and regularly see Brett and Steve Ella just about asleep. They would be sitting in a corner or lying on a rub-down table! How can you sleep an hour away from kick-off? Brett Kenny did it regularly.

Paul Taylor was the one who was always up for a bit of mischief. He lived the Central Coast, where I also lived. The Saturday morning training sessions we had were very hard because we started at 8.00 a.m. That meant I would leave the coast around 6.30 a.m. to get to Parramatta by 7.40 a.m. Paul would usually leave around 7.00 a.m! He would go past me somewhere on the motorway. As I was coming off the motorway near Parramatta I would see him pulled over by the police. One of the better things he was involved in was at a presentation night which we used to have around once a month. Ron Massey, the assistant, liked a 'feed', and Paul did this skit where he stuffed a couple of pillows up his T-shirt and started walking around all the garbage cans in Granville Park looking for food, giving the impression he was Massey.

Paul played full-back for me and sometimes we would move him up into the front line to give 'Stirlo' a rest at full-back when we were on defence. If I am not mistaken, I think Paul holds the record for the number of tackles made in a game for Parramatta at the new stadium. His photo is in the hall of fame for his forty-eight tackles in a game! And he was only tiny (not as big as Peter Stirling), but he was all action on the park come game time. The players were quite funny among themselves. I remember when the Crow retired, the youngster we brought in to replace him was christened 'The Sparrow', the hope being that he would grow into a Crow! Equally, Mark Laurie's nickname was Pebbles. His older brother, who was a star at the Roosters, was called Rocky, so when Mark arrived at the club they christened him 'Pebbles', hoping he would grow to be a boulder.

One incident which was not funny at the time again involved Eric Grothe. We were playing a semi-final at the Sydney Cricket Ground [SCG]. To warm up rugby league style, you needed to go out the back of the dressing sheds and across a little tarmac drive. Coming back from the warm-up, Eric slipped on the drive and could not go on. Luckily we had a reserve-grade game being played there as well, and a kid named Michael Erikson was playing. As he walked up the stairs at the end of the reserve-grade match, we had to turn him round and get him ready to play wing in that semi-final match.

The SCG had a fantastic atmosphere; it is difficult to describe really. As you got changed in those dressing-rooms you knew that the 'body-line series', Don Bradman, those sorts of events and people were involved in that stadium. It has a special place in the hearts and minds of all Australians who love sport. The whole place just affects you when you enter it. The sporting successes and failures it has witnessed make you feel a little humble when you get there. It was a place with a fantastic atmosphere, not just out on the paddock but in the dressing-rooms and the corridors. You know you are walking where great Australian sportsmen before you have walked, and it is just fantastic, a wonderful arena for any sport. I think the 1986 grand final was the last one played at that ground; it was just a fantastic place. I have to say it was much better than the late and unlamented Cumberland stadium we used to play at! That was an awful stadium really, rock-hard field with no grass on it during the winter time. A little caged area called the 'pig-pen' was where the coaches sat. There was a tiered set of three rows of wooden seats in the stand. Most people were glad when they burned it down during a party when we won the grand final!

Jack Gibson and Ron Massey also loved practical jokes and 'The Bear', Bob O'Reilly, was more often than not the butt of them. At one presentation evening they went out and bought the most expensive-looking watch case they could and then bought a $2 watch, both of which were gold-coloured. They got Michael Cronin to make the award to The Bear for some long-service thing. The Crow was always very sincere and made this wonderful speech saying how lucky the club was to have such a servant as The Bear. I think Bob suspected something, and that Jack and Ron might be behind it; he was not the most appreciative in his reply. Whereupon Ron Massey jumped up, ripped the watch out of his hands, calling him a mongrel, a big stupid front-row forward, telling him how ungrateful he was, all his team-mates had put in a great deal of money to buy the watch. With that, he proceeded to smash the watch on the table, which broke into a thousand pieces. The Bear was left standing there with just an expensive-looking case!

On another occasion, Jack and Ron somehow got hold of a piece of North Sydney Rugby League Club headed notepaper. It was at the time that that club was looking for a new coach. They sent a letter to The Bear inviting him to the League's club to be interviewed for the job. He turned up at the club asking to be directed to the interview, which no one there knew anything about!

The funny thing was that once the team went onto the paddock the frivolity ended. Steve Edge, the captain, would ensure that the game plan was followed right to the end of a game, even if we were twenty points behind. On the field it was work; the fun only came off the field.

One of the best one-liners I ever heard came from Jack Gibson. He, my wife Julie and I were up on the Gold Coast and went into a bar to get a drink. The guy behind the bar took an age to get to serving us. Finally, he turned and said, 'I will not keep you long.' Jack fixed him with a stare, as only Jack could, and said, 'You have already been long.' We got served!

That great side, though, was disintegrating. Towards the end, the chemistry was breaking down; it was time for Monie to move on and another coach to come in. Perhaps it is a measure of, first, Jack Gibson's achievements and then Monie's that, since those heady days of the early 1980s, the club has had little success. They have never been able to recreate the magic that existed in those days. Also, they have never been able to produce a championship-winning team. That is not to say they have not produced great players; they have. In the 1980s, however, they produced a great team. At the end of the 1989 season Monie bowed out. He had been there through the 1980s, which was the greatest period in the history of the Parramatta club. He left with a wealth of fond memories but, looking back, felt it was time to go. He sensed the board realised his time there was over and he had perhaps stayed too long. Although, as he pointed out, Wayne Bennett of the Brisbane Broncos seems to have disproved the point that a coach can stay too long. As Monie said, 'If the club is in good shape and your recruitment is right, then you can stay a long time.'

4

WIGAN FIRST TIME AROUND

'Do not seek personal glory, just do your job.'

When Maurice Lindsay introduced the new coach, John Monie, to the Wigan public it would be fair to say that there were a great many of them asking the question 'Why?'

That, in itself, is no surprise, simply because the average Wigan fan's interest in the affairs of other clubs stretches no further than what is happening at Knowsley Road, home of arch-rivals St Helens. In fact, the success of the Wigan club was, and still is, judged on beating the Saints, both at home and away if possible; championships and Challenge Cup wins are simply icing on the cake. So it was only to be expected that few fans would have heard of Monie.

The other question on the lips of the fans was, 'Will he be as good as Graeme Lowe?' Lowe, the coach who was leaving, was looked upon as a god by the fans. After all, he had brought back the glory days to the Central Park faithful. True, Lowe would be a hard act to follow, but what the fans did not realise was that Monie's task would be nowhere near as difficult as it had been at Parramatta in 1984, taking over from the great Jack Gibson. To Wigan fans, Gibson, like Monie, was an unknown factor. They would only enter Gibson or Monie into their psyche if they were to come and coach Wigan or St Helens; then, and only then, were they important.

It is little wonder that Monie had few worries about replacing Lowe; after all, he had previously replaced Jack Gibson, considered by many to be the best coach the game has seen. As Monie said:

> It was really down to my personality and philosophy on the game. I don't let things worry me, and after filling Jack Gibson's shoes, Lowe's were certainly not going to be any bigger. It did not stop people from telling me that I was on a hiding to nothing, though, for in their eyes, if the club did not continue along its successful path, people would point the finger at me. I was happy to live with that.

However, what did surprise him about England was the passion and feeling the fans had for their team. It was far and away greater than anything he had experienced back home.

> When I arrived at Central Park, I met fans who had sat in the same seat in the stand for thirty or forty years. There were groups of fans who stood on the same spot on the terraces every home game, and had been doing so for as long as they could remember. When I was up in the coach's gantry during a match I was completely switched off to everything around me other than the game itself. I did not realise just how much the crowd at Central Park actually chanted during the game, but this really came home to me during a match, probably in my second season with the club. There was a lull in the game and one of the stats guys said, 'Well, go on, then. Give 'em what they want.' I had not a clue what he was talking about until I stopped concentrating on the game and listened to the crowd on

> the far side of the ground. Almost to a man they were chanting, 'Monie, Monie, give us a wave.' It was the first time I had ever actually heard it; God only knows how long they had been chanting, probably since I had arrived I expect. I made the mistake of giving them a little wave and the reaction was deafening. You would have thought someone had scored the best try ever seen in a grand final! The roar that went up caused the players and officials on the paddock to stop and look up to see what was happening off the park. It is the sort of thing which does not happen in Australia and I cannot say why that should be. It just seems that passion is much more evident among the fans in England.

So it was that Monie arrived at Central Park, after nine years at Parramatta, with his batteries supposedly in need of recharging and contemplating a year off. This was to have been spent up the East Coast of Australia, surfing and relaxing, but it never materialised. The mortgage still had to be paid and food put on the table. Instead, even as he was clearing his desk at Parramatta stadium, he was firing off faxes to Graeme West, the reserve-grade coach at Wigan, to ensure pre-season work was following the lines he wanted:

> I never did get the break I was looking forward to. In fact, I spent the first month, or month and a half, of pre-season faxing plays, set pieces, names of players etc. over to 'Westy'. It was not so much a shock then for players when I arrived.
>
> The best thing that happened at Wigan was the strength of Ellery Hanley as the leader. A lot of those problems which bubble away under the surface at any club were solved because he was a good leader and a good captain. When I look back at any of the successful teams I have been involved in, I always look at the captain. I reckon nine out

of ten of those successful teams had a very dominant and mentally tough leader. That was what I had at Wigan in Ellery. He was then followed by Dean Bell, yet another physically and mentally tough guy. At Parramatta I had Steve Edge, then Ray Price, and finally Peter Stirling. They were all very tough people.

Finally, when I returned to Wigan in 1998, I had Andy Farrell, who was very young at the time. I saw an international player in Andy at a young age. At Wembley I dropped international Neil Cowie in order to put Farrell on the bench when he was only seventeen. I recognised the talent in Andy Farrell and he has gone on to be one of those leaders whom I always like to be associated with; they are a little bit special.

When I arrived at Wigan, as I said, Ellery made the job a little bit easier for me, simply because he was the leader of the pack and had an influence over everybody. I am not a pushy person, I assess things and have a look at what the existing situations are. Then, if I have any criticism I have it from an open book, as it were. It's the seventeen players and me sitting in the room. If I have something to say to every player, then every player listens to what I say. If they do not agree, then I want to hear about it.

Even at team meetings, if Ellery didn't agree with anything I said, he would question it and ask why I said a particular thing. He was just a great leader for the Wigan club at that time.

So, when I arrived a great deal was already in place, which didn't surprise me as I knew they were a great side, a great club and they had already had success. Although people said I did not change a great deal when I first arrived, I really already had! I sort of sneaked up on them and after six or eight weeks a lot of things had been changed around. The players had just not noticed it. One week I brought a new player in who had been playing reserve grade and whilst the players thought we were doing everything the same way, to the new guy coming in it was like another world. He just did not know what we were doing. I had sneaked it up on the first-grade players so it had become natural to them and even second nature. We had, in fact, progressed a fair bit in those eight weeks and had moved away from what was still happening in reserve grade, and consequently what had been happening under Lowe.

It took about half of that first season, or maybe even three-quarters, before the philosophy, methods and systems filtered through to the reserve grade and the under-19 youngsters. Only then were we able to bring the young kids into the top side, because by then the specific role they had to fill in top grade was similar to what they were already doing in lower-grade sides. It did become easier for young players to come into the first grade, but for the first three or four months I was there, the first-grade boys got way ahead of the other sides, simply because I could not have any input with them. It was like speaking English to reserve grade and Dutch to first grade. The two groups were on different wavelengths but the top grade went ahead in leaps and bounds.

It seems that Monie has always subscribed to the view that you need to get all the players at a club playing with the same philosophy. That is not to say that he stifled innovation from his reserve-grade coaches. He gave them complete freedom to coach the way they wanted, but they had to come within a framework containing his ideas for first grade. It was simply a matter of 'coach your own way', 'run the team how you want', but make sure my ideas are incorporated into your work. It was really a system which blended Monie's ideas from the top with whatever input and new ideas the fresh young coaches had.

It must be emphasised, though, that the major difference

Monie found on arrival at Wigan was the players' view that what was important was what they wanted, rather than what was good for the team. It was a philosophy he set about changing:

> I gradually wore them down; I just preached at the team all the time. What can I do for 'the team'? People don't realise how much time coaches and players spend together; it is probably more time than they spend at home with their families. Players have someone who is in charge, and they respect that person, and if that person doesn't deviate from the message that the team is the most important thing, then in the end they will think the way the coach thinks. I just bombarded them with my ideas and tried to get the best out of individuals so that they would help the team. It would always come back to the fact that the player had to be as good as was needed. All players have special talent, all can do something different from the next guy, and must be encouraged to use those different talents, in order to always help the team.

Not only did Monie have a new club and players to contend with when he arrived at the Wigan club, he was also faced with a different game. A game where, perhaps, the emphasis was more on attack than on defence:

> The game was a lot 'looser' than the Australian game when I arrived. The Aussie game was a lot more disciplined, harder to break down because there was not the freedom there. There was also not the intensity in England that was present down under, and, to be fair, it is probably still not to be found in the English game. There is intensity in the Wigan versus Saints or Bradford versus Leeds, those top-of-the-table clashes, but the intensity does drop away. That was one of the biggest weaknesses I found on my arrival.

From his earliest time at Central Park, in spite of the team having been coached by Lowe, who was knowledgeable about the Aussie game, the players still needed to lift their intensity. They also needed to improve their understanding of defensive systems and team defence. How could each player help his team-mate in the defensive line? As he put it:

> I wanted them to understand the system, as well as physically have to do it. It is one of my philosophies that players have to first understand the system mentally, intellectually or whatever. They have to understand what they are doing first, and then, physically, they have to go out and do it. They have to be able to do it when they are fatigued, when they are concussed, in fact under all sorts of different conditions. I once made the statement in my early coaching career that, 'The only reason you should not be in the defensive line is if you are unconscious. The moment your eyes open up you should be back on your feet, in the defensive line until such time as your team has the football and the medical people can get you off the field.' There is a real emphasis on physical toughness and that will lead to a mental toughness as well.
>
> At Wigan, in this respect, it was a matter of not deviating from what was needed to win the game. You had to be physically tough, mentally tough, and also to understand why you were doing it. It was never good enough for me that players did something well; they had to understand what they were doing. I think coaching is really teaching, and the way I coached was more about teaching. I wanted players to understand as much about the game when they finished their career as I understood about the game. I was also prepared to learn from players. If they did not like what I wanted and they had a better way of doing it, I listened to their ideas. A lot of my

players, from all eras of my coaching, even when I was coaching country football in Australia, have gone on to become coaches. I look back and am convinced it was because I wanted them to have an understanding of the game.

Monie quickly made an impression with the players both on and off the field. However, not only was he having to get the football side of things running the way he wanted, but he had to develop a working relationship with the chairman of Wigan, Maurice Lindsay, whom he knew little about. It was a relationship that moved quickly and, fortunately, in a positive way. It is no secret that the rapport which developed between them helped move the club on to a new level.

Maurice is a good judge of a footballer, but he does not try to coach. Sometimes you meet people within the game whom you automatically hit it off with, that you like, and you like the way they do their job. There is a mutual respect between you. I had not known Maurice for very long when I realised he would be a friend for life, simply because of our philosophy on life, and the things we liked. Neither of us had great interests outside of the game, but those we did have were very strong and similar. Straightaway there was a symbiosis, a mutual respect.

It was that respect which carried the club forward, simply because Lindsay could see what Monie was doing and was happy with what he saw. On the other hand, Monie could see what his chairman was doing and was equally happy. Monie was informed very early that the club would leave no stone unturned to get players who would strengthen the club. Both were working to make Wigan as strong as possible. A lot of people would say they overstepped the mark at times.

Monie inherited a club but did not sit back and rest on his

laurels; he set about building the club up, not just the first grade, but the club as a whole. He was equally clear just how that was going to be achieved:

> When you look back on anything which turned out to be great, you see that you set your own standards. The first thing Maurice and I agreed on was that we did not want to use any other club as our benchmark. We wanted to set our own standards and I wanted the players to set their own standards. We never said, 'This is the way they do it at this club or that club.' We said, 'We will set our own benchmark. We will raise the bar as high as we want to raise it.' We did not want to raise our standards just so that we could win at the end of the season, although that was one of our goals. We did not want to be held back by anyone. We decided we were going to do something special at this club and we were not going to use any other club as our benchmark. We had no idea where it would take us or where it would stop; that philosophy would take us wherever it took us.

People, as is always the case, concentrate on the first-grade teams at Wigan, which I suppose is only natural. Monie, however, took great pride in the fact that many of those players in reserve grade went on to play first grade at Wigan and other clubs. He always believed you could never have an outstanding first-grade side unless you had great recruitment and great development of the junior talent in your club. If you were to shoot for the sky, so to speak, you could not do it with one football side. There had to be reserve-grade sides in the slipstream, as well as under-19 sides. It was then a case of dragging everything to new heights. As Monie said:

> There were guys like Michael Forshaw, who could not make

> the side in that era, who went on to become one of the better players in a very strong Bradford outfit, week in and week out. The standards were set in those years, and the youngsters in the reserves who were learning alongside those first-grade players, even when they did not break into the first grade, went on to become very good first-grade players with other clubs. They were not making it at the time the great Wigan side was, but their time was to come. I am sure the lessons they learned and the habits they developed in that era helped them further down the track.

One of the qualities which quickly endeared Monie to the Wigan club and its fans was his belief that everyone in the club was important; all helped the team to succeed. In his eyes everyone had a part to play, a job to do, and he made everyone at the club aware of that fact. People, regardless of the job they did, were to be treated with respect and courtesy. Players treated everyone with the same respect they gave the coach or the chairman. It was, again, a job of educating people; what was important was the team and no matter how lowly the job, if it did not get done the team could not win. It was a case of the chain only being as strong as its weakest link!

One of the important aspects of Monie's stint at Wigan, which tends to be overlooked, was the quality of the imports he brought into the club. He did not pluck them out of the air, rather a great deal of time and effort went into finding the player who could best strengthen the team.

> My philosophy was to try to bring in good players. Maurice Lindsay changed that by saying, 'Keep your eyes on what we are trying to do here. Don't worry about the money side of things. If we are going to import players, we are going to bring in champion players.' We were always aware of positions where we would be losing a top-flight player, and the recruitment was always geared to where we needed to

strengthen further down the track. The prerequisite was to bring people in who could do something I could not coach!

One such player was Gene Miles, whom Monie had the utmost respect for.

> Gene was a pearl, just fantastic. He could do things that a lot of people could not coach; Martin Offiah could do things you could never coach. When Offiah came to Wigan, his speed was so good I saw him at Shaun Edwards' testimonial day outrun an Olympic athlete over 100 metres.

Martin Offiah was perhaps the last piece in the jigsaw that completed the greatest Wigan team of Monie's era at the club. Getting him to the club was, in Monie's eyes, the best piece of business Lindsay ever did:

> There is no doubt it was Maurice who got him to the club from under the nose of Leeds. Maurice had been talking to Martin for some time when, one afternoon, Martin rang him at home and told him he had decided to go to Leeds. Maurice had to think on his feet so asked where he was speaking from. Offiah was driving back from Leeds to Widnes, so Maurice invited him to stop off on the way to have a coffee with him at home.
>
> Maurice had no sooner put the phone down when it rang again, and Doug Laughton, the Leeds coach, began gloating to him, 'I've got Martin at Leeds. You have finally lost one, little man,' said Doug, who was a friend of Maurice's. He listened while Doug told him he had never really had a chance, after all, Doug had brought him to Widnes in the first place. Also his good friend Ellery Hanley was already at the Leeds club. Maurice duly listened, saying very little, certainly not letting him know Offiah had just

rung! At the end he quietly put the phone down.

Offiah duly arrived and sat in the library while the chairman got him a soft drink. Taking the coffee and soft drink in, he was greeted by Offiah commenting in the numerous books and videos on rugby which were on the shelves. It was then that he pulled off the master stroke, as far as I was concerned.

'I don't know what it is about Wigan fans but they just love wingers,' he started to say. 'We have had some great ones, Billy Boston, Trevor Lake, Henderson Gill. I don't know what it is about the Spion Kop end of Central Park, but you know there will be 18,000 supporters there, and when a wing man scores at that end it's as if the whole crowd is pulling him into their bosom.'

I looked at Offiah and he was hooked. Maurice began to reel him in. 'You will do well at Leeds, Martin; they are a good club. Mind you, the in goal is so short there when you score, with your speed you will probably run right over the crowd as well. Pity, the Spion Kop crowd at Central Park would have loved to see you scoring there for them!'

'Well, I have not signed for Leeds yet, you know,' said Martin.

Maurice had him, and he then did the hardest thing: he shut up and let Offiah drink his coke and leave.

A couple of days later Offiah rang Maurice to say he wanted to come to Wigan but the club would have to sort it out with Jim Mills, the Widnes chairman. I was at Maurice's house when they were negotiating over the phone. They were on for hours. I lost count of the number of times I must have gone out of the room to make a cup of coffee, walk around the house and come back in! Maurice was still on the phone trying to hammer out a deal with Jim Mills. Some of the figures which were being bandied about made me look at Maurice, roll my eyes and back out of the room again.

I do know that Jack Robinson had put a ceiling on how high Maurice could go in the negotiations. They told him not a penny more than £400,000. In the end he overruled them and did the deal with Mills at £440,000. But it took a very long time! I never did find out if Doug Laughton rang Maurice again once he found out he had lost Offiah. The 'little man', as he usually did, had won the day once again.

We paid so much for Offiah simply because we both knew he would take the football team to a new level. Like all players, he had strengths and he had weaknesses, and it was my job not to camouflage his weaknesses but to turn them into acceptable strengths. We also had to make him want to lift his game and become a better player.

When any player came into the Wigan club, they saw how hard all the others, who were champion players, worked. They also saw how much 'being great' meant to them. That quickly rubbed off on new players who arrived at the club. They had to jump in, boots and all, to reach that high standard. But then, what they could do, which I could not coach, was that little bit which took the team to another level.

I think Offiah was in shock for a little while when he arrived, but like all champion players, and he was one of those, he had that air of confidence about him. We had paid £440,000 for him, and on one of the first training sessions up on the top training pitch behind Central Park I thought we had lost him! At one end of the paddock the field goes from grass, to sand, to dirt, to concrete. Martin got on the end of one of our back-line moves and was flying. Before he knew it he had run off the grass, the sand and the dirt onto the concrete with his boots on! He landed on his stomach and slid along the concrete patch for a while and then just lay there!

The whole training session stopped. Andy Platt ran over,

looked down at him, started to laugh and turned to look at me and said, 'What a waste of money – we've killed him in the first training session!' With that, Martin did half a push-up and jumped to his feet, realising, he wasn't going to get any sympathy.

He did have that air of confidence all champions have; it is part of the package which makes them great but they were certainly brought back into the fold when they came to Wigan.

There was at the time a player who you most certainly could not bring back into the fold easily, if at all – Andy Gregory.

Andy was fantastic and moody. If something had happened which he did not like or if a player did not come onto the ball when Andy wanted him to, his training would drop down a peg or two for the next five minutes. It stayed like that until someone ran past him and gave him a pat and said, 'Come on, Greg.' I would say, 'Let me see how you did that play again, mate, the way you put that ball out there, let me see you do that again,' and he would go. The ball would fly out and Andy Goodway would come onto it. I would say what fantastic play it was and Greg was away again, on top of the world.

Andy's peaks were very high and his valleys very low, so when he got down on himself and he felt he was in the dumps, he certainly was low and did not like it. He did not like me replacing him in a game either. We would put Bobby Goulding on for the last ten minutes or so of a game. The first time I did it, I can remember him looking up into the coaches' box, which was very obvious at Central Park. The players know exactly where it is and many times after we had scored a try Greg would run under the box, look up and ask what kick-off drill we should run. When I sent the message down 'Get Greg off and put Goulding on' this day, he ran over, spread out his arms and said, 'Me – you want to bring me off?'

There is a great Greg story about the time when I replaced him at Old Trafford in a Challenge Cup semi-final against St Helens. Robin Whitfield was the referee and Greg was fighting with him right from the word go, right from first kick-off. We were down in the first half; Greg was giving away penalty after penalty and extra tens for back chat and would not back off the referee. Equally the referee would not back off him; both of them had the stubborn streak in them. In the end I had had enough and sent the message to get him off!

It was ten minutes before half-time when we put Goulding on. Greg came off and instead of sitting on the bench he ran up the tunnel. I walked down at half-time into the dressing-room and sensed there was something not right in the dressing-room. I could see Andy Gregory was not in there. I asked where he was and Westy said, 'Mate, you have never seen anything like it. When the band marched on at half-time, he was sitting in the middle of the tunnel, halfway down. The whole band had to walk round him as he sat there. The players had to walk round him; he just sat there!'

Westy asked if he should go and get him and I told him to leave him where he was. As the band came off they had to walk round him again.

About fifteen to twenty minutes into the second half the game was tight and I said, 'Someone go into the tunnel and get Greg. Tell him we need him; we need to win this game.' The crowd on the other side of the stadium could obviously see part way down the tunnel because this big roar went up. I thought, 'What is that all about?' Next thing Greg came out of the tunnel like a little cannonball.

Towards the end of the game, Ellery made a break and put Andy Goodway in for a try under the posts which took us to Wembley. Greg is fantastic, a good friend of mine, and I really enjoy his company. When you are around him, you are always laughing.

It must be said that Monie was blessed, or cursed, with yet another funny guy in his team; the hooker, Martin Dermot. If Gregory was the clown prince, then Dermot most definitely was the court jester.

A great character was Dermot. When I got to Wigan the hooker was Nicky Kiss, a very good, tough player. He was coming to the end of an era, and the new hookers did not need to be as tough as Nicky. Martin Dermot's dummy half work, which was all off the floor, was real precision. When he ran out of dummy half he could make something happen. That was the hard part of coaching; coming into a club and looking at a guy sitting in reserve grade who was the sort of hooker you wanted. At the same time you have a guy in first grade who has tremendous admiration from everyone in the club. He has paid the price, done everything for the club. I knew instantly, though, that Nicky Kiss was not my hooker; Martin Dermot was.

Graeme West did not agree. I did not have a lot of arguments with people but that was one of them. He felt Dermot would let me down, he was not as tough as Kiss, he could not do this, he could not do that. But there was never any doubt in my mind Martin Dermot was to be the first-grade hooker.

He was one of those practical jokers in the dressing-room. I often walked into the dressing-room before a big game, or at half-time, and if the players were all laughing I would say, 'Derms, I've told you not to do that!' He would reply, 'Why do you always blame me?' I would answer, 'If something has happened in this room and I blame you, I am never far off the truth.' Nine times out of ten I was right.

One time he nearly cut his arm off when he fell over in the shower. The players told me he had slipped in the shower and the soap holder had hit his elbow on his way through and smashed. The jagged edges had cut his arm very badly. I thought to myself, 'I bet he was fooling around at the time.' I never found out, but I bet I am not far off the truth saying that he was skylarking in the shower. He was fun, and always great to have in the team.

Monie could tell a player that his time was up, but did it with dignity and logic and reasoned argument. As he admits, it is one of the downsides of the job. It was a tough time and each player had to be handled differently. Monie felt Kiss was a real man about everything he did. There was never any animosity, even though there was a great deal of disappointment, and Kiss accepted the decision had been made and could see the reasons for it. Monie said:

I had the same problem when I dropped Shaun Wane from the side. Shaun said to me, 'When Graeme Lowe came he dropped me from the side after a month, now you have been here a month and you are dropping me from the side.' He asked me why I had dropped him, and I took him into the office and told him. 'Two weeks ago you got tackled and lost the ball three times. I told you then that it was not acceptable; it is your responsibility to hang on to the ball. Last week you lost the ball in the tackle twice more.' Shaun looked at me bewildered and asked if that was the only reason and I told him, yes. He said, 'Well, I can do something about that.' I told him to put it right in reserve grade and when it was right he would get back in first grade.

Shaun was a player who did not train hard enough to play the way he wanted to play on match days. I always use Andy Platt as an example. Andy played the way Shaun

> played, which was to hold nothing back, whatever he had he unloaded on match day. Andy, though, trained to play that way, whereas Shaun didn't train hard enough to play the way he wanted. That is a lesson for younger players to take note of. Everyone wants to give their all on match day; I don't think there is anyone playing this game who does not want to give their all, and more. Shaun Wane wanted to do this but his body kept breaking down because he did not prepare it. He did not want to 'go beyond' during the week, in training. Andy Platt did this whilst getting ready, and then went beyond again during the game. Shaun did it on Sundays but kept getting hurt simply because his body could not stand up to what he was asking of it.

The job has its downside in as much as coaches have to tell players that their time at a club is up. Another problem is when players leave although the coach doesn't want to lose them. During his time at Wigan Monie faced two such situations, with the loss of Ellery Hanley and Andy Gregory.

> I was very disappointed at the time when Ellery left the club. I had my say with Maurice Lindsay about it along with the other board members. I would not want people to think that I agreed with everything Maurice did, far from it. If I felt the wrong decisions were being made, I told him so. He was man enough to accept that and often we would agree to differ. Maurice brought the Ellery thing back to a business decision. The facts and figures were simple; the club could get a good price for Ellery from Leeds, we had Phil Clarke playing in our second team, he was going to be the next Great Britain lock. It was felt the club would not miss out too much if Ellery left, although Maurice did not say that because, as I pointed out, Ellery was a champion, a once-in-a-lifetime player and you just don't let players like that leave your club. You get everything out of them you

can! But that was from my side of the job. Maurice, from his side said there was a time to sell, when the price was good. Had we waited another season or two the financial balancing may well not have been good business. It was a business decision to let Ellery go at the end of the day. As it turned out Clarke did become the next GB lock and played some good seasons for the club.

With Andy Gregory that was just a tragedy; Jack Robinson made a lot of silly decisions. In fairness, though, he did sign Frano Botica, and even though it was a decision I did not agree with at the time, it turned out to be a great one. So you are not right as a coach all the time. If I had been in the country I think we could have resolved the situation, and got another season or two out of Andy Gregory.

A football team operates around its half-back, there is no getting away from that. If you want to win a competition or have a champion team, you have to have a champion half-back. Andy Gregory-type players might come along once every twenty years or so, or it could even be once in a lifetime. In the English game I have not seen a half-back who was, or is, as good as Andy. They tell me Alex Murphy was the greatest half-back in England, but I never saw him play. From the tape I have seen on Murphy he was a guy who could run the football with lightning acceleration whereas Andy was a ball player extraordinaire; it was a joy to watch him play!

Jack Robinson, the Wigan chairman, signed Frano Botica from New Zealand rugby union, much against the wishes of his coach. But Botica did become a record points-scorer for the club. Monie had nothing against the player; in fact, when faced with the decision, he simply set about coaching him to play rugby league. Monie's argument was simply, 'Why take a risk?'

I told Jack at the time why take a risk with a rugby union player? I had a guy, Phil Blake, who had proved himself in the Australian game. With the skills he had and the way he played he would have been a sensation in the English game. We had him on loan, along with Les Davidson, for a twelve-week period when Adrian Shelford and Kevin Iro were out of the country playing for New Zealand. The way Phil played the game was sensational, so why take a risk when you don't have to? My point was not as a knock on Botica, but, rather, we should not have to take these risks. There is already a player we can sign who is a champion player.

Once Botica was signed, it was my job to coach and make him the best rugby league player I could. I introduced him to the game by playing him on the wing. There, he only had to do what a wing man does (players who hang around football teams but don't contribute much!), but it was better than sitting in the stand. He was close enough to the action to see what went on around first and second receivers' roles, the intensity of the forward clashes and when the ball should go to the backs. He was like an observer out on the wing for months and when I felt the time was right he was moved closer to the action at six or seven. He turned out to be an exceptionally good goal-kicker.

He was one of those guys who practised kicking all the time. He told me that he could not get into the All Blacks side because Grant Fox, one of the all-time leading points-scorers for that country, played the same position. 'Botts' could not get in because Fox was just a phenomenal goal-kicker, but he realised then that it was one way to cement your place in a team. I think he just decided he had the technique and the timing, and it was all about practice. He was going to practise longer and harder than the other goal-kickers. He made himself into the kicker he became. It may well come back to the Wigan thing, seeing all the other players working really hard at their own skills and working hard at the things which were going to help the team. He would come in early before training started and practise goal-kicking.

His wife, Tracy, would collect the balls and get them back to him to kick again. If the weather was bad and we were training at the Robin Park complex, he would practise indoors. He used to roll up an old football sock to make a kicking tee and kick into a shot putt net from the indoor running track. Technique and timing were what mattered; he only kicked the ball two metres before it hit the net. To him, it was all about his timing and preparation.

He became an expert in converting four pointers into six pointers. I even got to know his range particularly well. Bob Lanigan, who worked with us and had been with me for years, used to show me how far he could kick. When 'Lanno' was over at Wigan he would take the kicking tee out and a lot of times, with Bobby Goulding as well as Frano if we had scored in the corner, I would see him actually run to a different spot from where they were stood with the ball. He would go closer to the try-line, then he would come back and say, 'He was too far back, he would have missed the crossbar by a metre.' Bobby Goulding would always want to go back a couple more metres to get a better angle on the posts; Lanno would move him up. I have seen Frano hit the crossbar when Lanno had said they were right on the limit of their range.

Like everything at the club it was about everyone pulling together to help the team to win the football game on a Sunday.

Whatever it was, it worked. Come Sunday, more often than not, the team walked off the paddock as winners. During Monie's first spell at the club they won all that there was to win. There were spectacular matches won in spectacular fashion, but they did not simply happen. It was a case of good planning, good preparation and good execution, not good luck, that won Monie's men so many matches.

5

THE BIG GAMES AT WIGAN

'Few things are as painful as an invisible wound.'
– Nelson Mandela

It as always been Monie's belief that winning is not just about the thirteen guys on the pitch. At Wigan, under Monie, it was always much more than that; it was the fifteen or the seventeen who took part in the match. It was the rest of the squad, who may well have made contributions during the week's preparation for the game. It was about the medical staff who had treated injuries to a degree where the player could get out on the field. For Monie, it was always an effort by the team for the team. It was a philosophy which worked and saw the club reach new heights and set new standards in the English game.

When he arrived at Wigan he set about winning games, but in the early days was pleasantly surprised by the way the competition in England was set up.

> Because I am Australian I am a big fan of the grand final approach; I feel it is the right way to go and it brings a season to a great climax. However, many times the best team in the competition, and the most consistent team in the competition, never make it to the grand final, let

alone win it. So when I arrived I was pleasantly surprised with the system here. You play thirty games in a season and whoever wins the most is the champion of the league.

Whilst I like the grand final system, the English system made a lot of sense to me. Over a period of thirty or forty weeks, with cup comps and all, the more you win, the harder it is to be champion because everyone is shooting at you, and putting greater strain on you. I just thought it was a great system! When I returned in 1998 I was only glad we did finish in first place and we did win the grand final, because we were the most consistent team. We got the big reward but we could easily not have done.

Monie had been involved with two grand finals during his time at Parramatta; now he was to meet the English equivalent. In his first season in charge he took the club to Wembley stadium for his first Rugby League Challenge Cup final. You would think such an event would not faze the experienced coach, but he found it the most amazing experience of his life:

It was an outstanding, unbelievable, emotional day out. At the time, though, it was difficult. It is not that I was not enjoying it; I was aware of what was going on, of the emotion of the day, of the hundred thousand people there at that first final against Warrington. The noise when we walked out onto the pitch was actually so loud it was almost physical in the way it hit you. It made you take a step back or take an extra big gulp of air because it was on top of you and around you. I have never known anything like the atmosphere in that Wembley stadium in my whole coaching career. A superb, super-duper day.

I remember two things about that final as clear as if they were happening today. One was that Adrian Shelford blew a tap play early in the game, which he should not have done. He forgot his assignment, which always bugs me as a coach, and he was in the wrong place at the wrong time. The other was Mark Preston's intercept try which went ninety metres down one side line, straight as a gun barrel. Then he scored another one. These are the things which stand out for me.

Selling him after this final was not because of his ability to do his job, but we were taking the team to another level. His first try against Warrington at Wembley is one of my fondest memories of that final.

When we played St Helens at Wembley in 1991 and beat them 13–8, Ellery was really struggling. Doctor Zamon had needled his hamstring, but Ellery got on the park and played an inspirational role in us winning again. That was a Wembley final we should not have won! We were held together by sticking plaster and needles, we had no right to win that game. Somehow, giving all credit to the players, they physically got the job done. It was a test of their mental strength ensuring they could go out and physically do it. That was a tough one! I have no doubt it was because Ellery was out there; he did some things above the call of duty that day. If we were ever going to lose one, that was the one. You had to be disappointed if you were associated with St Helens that day; it should have been their cup.

Another inspiration that day, as he had been the year before when he remained on the field against Warrington after sustaining a shattered eye socket, was Shaun Edwards. Monie had the utmost respect for his half-back.

Shaun's father, Jacky Edwards, was single-minded about his son being a rugby league player and gave him the pushes in the right directions. He helped him with his training when he was a youngster. Shaun himself developed that single-mindedness, which took him to heights leading him to become the most decorated player in the English game.

Whereas Andy Gregory had a talent which was a real gift, Shaun was to my mind a little more like Dennis Betts. You would not say either of them had one thing which was a real gift, that other players didn't have. But they manufactured a way to greatness through hard work, through planning. They are probably the sportsmen you have to admire the most: they were single-minded, had a plan, physically did everything in their power to become a champion player. Shaun developed tactical awareness, developed his kicking game; he was always working on his game. It has not surprised me that, now he has retired, he has won more in the English game than any other player. Against Warrington in 1990, though, he showed his courage to carry on playing with a horrific injury until the job was done.

It was not just finals which saw Monie with his players perfectly prepared. One game which still highlights his unique ability was the cup semi-final annihilation of Bradford by a record score of 71 points to 10. It was a game most who witnessed will never forget. To Monie, it was simply his team getting the job done.

That game was like any other semi-final you go into. You are edgy because it is the Challenge Cup. One slip-up and you are gone. Wigan had built up this fantastic run of cup wins and had not missed a beat, as it were. Like the players, I had worked hard to ensure we were well prepared and knew where to attack them. I have always tried to prepare a team for the opposition and make sure nothing happened on the field which was not expected to happen. With that Wigan side, I concentrated on being sure they would not encounter something that I had not prepared them for.

I used to go over the tapes pretty thoroughly and then we would decide what we thought Bradford, or whoever, were going to do. We would run it against each other in training, half the team against the other half, so, when they went out on match day, whatever happened the players had seen it before. That was one of the edges we had.

Then Andy Greg, Gene Miles, Offiah, Bell and those sort of guys did the rest. To a man, the whole squad was on the money against Bradford in that semi-final. As we were walking off the field at half-time, Greg waited until he was within earshot of Peter Fox, the Bradford coach. He then turned to Joe Lydon and in a loud voice said, 'Joe, I think we should declare and send them in!' I can remember how excited Greg was when he came off the field, not about the score but because they were going back to Wembley. Again, we were setting our own standards, we knew how we wanted to work and how hard we wanted to work. Sometimes, funny as it seems, the opposition did not have anything to do with the way we were going to play. They weren't going to surprise us with anything they were going to do, and did not affect how we would play the game. So intense and insular were our preparations I don't think people in the game really understood what we were doing.

One day the referee came to me after the match and said, 'I heard Andy Gregory say they were going to run a three by three off the next ruck. What the hell was all that about?' We probably were a step ahead of everybody at that time with our game plans.

Monie's time at Wigan was all about setting new heights and the gods conspired to give him the opportunity to see just how high his achievements could rise. It was not at thirteen-a-side, though, but rather in the form of the World Seven-a-side competition in Sydney. When the invitation dropped on the mat at Central Park, it was too good an opportunity to miss for Monie and his chairman, Maurice Lindsay.

> The weather was cyclonic down there when we played. It was a risk which we probably should not have taken because the week we returned we were due to go straight into the Challenge Cup; a black and white sort of comp where you are alive or you are dead. It was a huge risk!
>
> Sevens football is one of those things where you participate and it is a bit of a lark and fun. It was back in Australia, which was a great trip and we were going to have a lot of fun. But then, if you win, it suddenly, becomes a serious competition. You look back at the Wigan trophy cabinet, and there it is, the World Sevens trophy. Suddenly, it is more than a good trip and a lot of fun; it's a serious comp and we won!
>
> We were very lucky to win it, and we thought we had gone out in the second round. By some mysterious count-back system, which saw us being beaten by fewer points than another club had been beaten by, we got through. So it was that Maurice came to the hotel and told me, 'We are progressing to the next round of the competition.' We had players scattered everywhere and I remember Maurice back at the hotel saying, 'You'd better go and find the players: we are still alive and are on again tomorrow.' I was chasing guys out of bars and betting shops, and making phone calls to find them!
>
> The Aussies hated it when we won. They could not believe a Pommie team had come over and beaten the best of the Aussie teams and the best the rest of the world had to offer. It was Martin Offiah and Gene Miles who did the damage, but again you can go through the names; we had great players. Andy Gregory did not want to go, he felt he was not suited to sevens. I think he wanted the trip, but felt

sevens football was not his style. Once he knew he was part of my plans for the comp, and I told him he could be fantastic in this game, he revelled in it! On a tape I saw of the comp, Greg Hartley described him as 'a little pommie with milk-bottle legs'.

The casualty out of the whole event was David Myers, the other wing man we took. He did not realise it at the time, but every time Martin Offiah scored a try I brought him off. I put David on, which meant the opposition got the ball from the kick-off, and David defended until we got the ball back, when I put Martin on again. Come the end of the second day, David Myers was shattered. He had not scored a try and was completely fatigued! He was doing sprint practice up and down the hallway of the Hilton Hotel in Sydney because he thought he had lost his pace. He had not worked out the fact that he had been used on defence and to chase back and get kicks. Poor old David Myers – he was a shattered man!

In the end the Aussie press gave credit where it was due. They saluted Gene Miles and Dean Bell. Martin Offiah was the man of the series. They held their hands up and said, 'You have some great players.'

When we won I was happy for Wigan more than for myself; happy for the players. It was not a personal thing; you should not coach for personal glory in my view. Those sevens, though, will stay in my memory for ever. I have to smile when I think we beat Brisbane in the final, and yet the night before we had had a bonding party with them up in Maurice's suite at the hotel, never dreaming we would meet them in the final!

The big games that the club won in this period did not happen by chance. Monie would also be the first to agree – they did not happen solely because of his efforts and skills. What comes shining through when you spend time with Monie is the loyalty he expects, some would say demands, from his players and coaching staff. He sees this as a two-way process, feeling they expect loyalty from him. Giving and receiving that loyalty is something that he prides himself on.

> I like to keep players together. A lot of coaching is my judgement on players and I do not like to lose good players. Once I work with good players I like to stay loyal to them till the end. That is why the Steve Hampson episode at Wigan left a sour taste in my mouth. Here was a player who had gone beyond the call of duty many times, won big games for the club. What the club did to him when his testimonial year came up was disgraceful. [Hampson was cut from the Wigan squad by the Wigan chairman Jack Robinson while he was on holiday and found out about the situation via the press. Monie always felt that Hampson had a couple of years left in the team at the top level. The fact that Hampson was due a testimonial year could well have had some bearing on the decision to drop him.]
>
> The same thing happened to Andy Gregory when I went to Australia to try to re-sign Gene Miles. When I got back, 'Greg' had been sold to Leeds. Those sorts of things bug me. You might wait twenty years for another Andy Gregory to come along again, and then only if you are lucky. So, as I said earlier, when you get great players to work with, you want to work with them for as long as you possibly can.

Andy Gregory was in discussions with the Wigan chairman, Robinson, about a new contract. It seems the chairman became impatient with the way events were unfolding and offered Gregory for transfer, an offer that was rapidly accepted by coach Doug Laughton at Leeds. Monie lost his number-one half-back because the chairman lost his patience! It is fair to say that problems of this nature seem to arise only in England and as a result of the different ways club chairmen operate in the two countries.

> The chairmen over in England have a completely different role from those in Australia. Chairmen in Australia look after the running of the football club and do not interfere with the rugby league side of things. Over in England most of the chairmen fancy themselves as good judges of players and start sticking their noses into areas they shouldn't.

Monie would, however, exempt the former Wigan chairman Maurice Lindsay from that criticism to a large extent:

> Do not for one minute think that Maurice and I always agreed, or that I was simply a 'yes' man. That was not the case; we disagreed on many occasions but had enough respect for each other's ability to come to some sort of agreement. Maurice, however, did not interfere much in the rugby league side of things. The other thing was that he *was* a good judge of a player and people tend to sell him a bit short in that regard. He always had opinions on players, and when you checked the player out, you found his opinion was never far off the mark. Coaches have to be able to judge players and there are some people who will tip you off; Maurice was a good judge. He would always get around things the right way, too. He could get you batting his way when you did not realise it!

People often wonder about how top coaches go about building a great team or squad and developing the loyalty between players and their coach. Do they develop a game plan they want to play to, and then find the players to fit around that plan? Do they look at the players available and then devise a game plan to suit those players at the club? Monie is in no doubt as to what should be done.

> I think you have to recognise the talent first, although you do need to have a fair idea also of what you are trying to do. When you move to a club, you need to work out what has been there, what its strengths are. Then you try to build your team around what you have got. There are key areas; every team has to have an outstanding half-back. You have always to be strong up front. You have to have speed in your back line. You need guys who can score tries for you out on the wings. Those are prerequisites which are pretty obvious. Primarily, though, you need talent; talent is the bottom line. It doesn't matter who you are or what you are doing, if you haven't got talent or the individuals to take charge of things come three o'clock on Sunday, then you are going to be in trouble.

Unfortunately, with talent comes ego; generally speaking, it is as certain as night follows day. Monie had talented players capable of winning big games at both Parramatta and at Wigan, yet he seemed to be able to balance those players' egos to ensure that the teams continued to be successful.

> Yes, I think that was a major achievement for me. At Wigan from 1992 to 1994 we did okay. I don't think there is ever a club at which you do not have trouble with players, but I have always managed to keep that trouble 'in-house', as it were. At Wigan any difficulties we kept between Maurice, or later Jack, the player and myself, and it did not go any further. We had plenty of problems, believe me, but it stayed our business. It did not affect the team, it did not affect training sessions and generally it did not get into the papers. That's an art in itself, you know. It was the same at Parramatta; things were dealt with and always kept between myself and the players and rarely got into the press.
>
> One of the things I noticed very early in my time in

England was that the English were more temperamental and harder to work with. The Aussies were more professional about team situations, about the requirements of playing for each other and that sort of thing. I have always found the English players a little more 'me' than 'we'; they were always a little more focused on themselves than on the team. At Parramatta I felt the bottom line was always coming back to 'How can I help the team?' 'What have I got to do to help the team?' 'Did the team win because of the way I played?' There was a responsibility for the players to be as good as they could be as individuals, but the underlying thing was always 'the team'.

As I said earlier, it was an approach I took from Parramatta over to Wigan and tried to foster. We certainly tried it with the first team. 'If the team wins, we all win,' was the philosophy I advocated. It is a philosophy which is important regardless of how the individual has played. Some weeks it may well be a different four or six who have good games and two or four guys who didn't perform well. If the team wins you carry those two or four who had an off week or did not play to their potential. If the team wins it always covers up the shortcomings which individuals have got. That is one of the theories I have always worked on. If everybody puts the team first, you will have success.

Dean Bell always felt that under Monie's coaching the team hated losing more than they liked winning, and as Monie is reaching the end of his coaching career, he is, he feels, better able to expand on that belief.

As I got to the last few years of my coaching career, the feeling I got when we lost was greater and more intense than the joy I got from winning. When we win I still feel good about it, but the good feeling is not as great as the bad feeling I get when we lose. That is probably a carry over from the philosophy I had at Parramatta, at Wigan and even at Auckland. In order to have those feelings it is important to have the loyalty of the players, which only comes if the players recognise the loyalty you have for them.

I think it was probably that loyalty which made me stay at Wigan longer than I had intended. Maurice convinced me to stay another year and see if we could keep the club going forward. Then the news broke that he was moving to become the chief executive of the Rugby League. He wanted to try and lift the game in England, try to do for the English game what he had done for Wigan. He was, I feel, so successful in his role there that he probably became perhaps the most disliked bloke in rugby league! He was successful, and it is a common trait in all sports that if you are too successful you get knocked. But he wanted to improve the standing of the game and look at the bigger picture.

He asked me, as a favour, if I would stay for another year (my fourth) while Jack Robinson settled into the job of chairman. Because of my friendship with Maurice, and quite a bit of money, I stayed that fourth season. It was different dealing with Jack. We had a very successful season on the rugby league side, but there was a breakdown between what Jack was trying to do and what we had already done! I actually made a prediction to Maurice Lindsay that Jack could not ruin the club in one year, but he would certainly set it back in two years. Jack had been in the shadow of Maurice, in the background, so to speak. He wanted to step into the limelight, and I cannot blame him for that. I have no bad feelings towards him, even though he certainly attacked me in the press when I left the club. He was really just trying to get his slice of the cake. He wanted to have a go, so he did what he did.

The first job he did, which he blew, related to Gene Miles. I was in Australia trying to talk Gene into coming

> back, but Jack, in England, decided he was too old and was talking to Andrew Farrar. Andrew Farrar was, however, a success story; he played great rugby league for Wigan. He may not have been Gene Miles, but he certainly was a very tough competitor. I feel I got him to play some of his best rugby league and he admitted that he did things in his days at Wigan which he had been unable to do in his Sydney career. He came to us from the Western Suburbs, but he had been in those very strong Canterbury sides of that time, so his background was right. So it was a case of getting the best out of Andrew, and I developed a long friendship with him. He is another one of my players who went on to be a first-grade coach!

The players also saw a different side to the club with Jack in charge. Gone were the extravagant bonuses Maurice was famous for. Some would say Maurice was too generous; Jack most certainly was not. The win bonuses were a lot less under Robinson than they had been in previous seasons.

It is difficult for Monie to say which was the best Wigan performance during those fabulous four years at the club. He himself said that he was so caught up in the game itself at the time that he never really had an objective opinion of the whole performance.

> I have never been one to rate games or rate seasons. I think the best of the Wigan sides during my time was that when Gene Miles was here. We beat Bradford by the big score, we also beat Leeds in a championship semi-final by a big score, when Offiah, who played outside Miles, crossed for ten tries. Looking back, it is hard to recall a game clearly but incidents in games stick in my mind, like Preston's intercept try at Wembley. I remember Offiah scoring against Castleford from a Shaun Edwards kick. I reckon the Castleford boys had twenty metres on Martin but over sixty

metres he picked up those twenty. I remember Ellery at Bolton making a break and running sideways leaning on someone, that was against Saints. You remember bits of games more than full games.

If I had to pick a match it would be the game in 1998 in the play-off against Leeds. It was played in the rain but we decided we were going to play football even though the conditions were against it. We beat them by a good score and we played some football, in the rain, in both halves. That goes against my grain a little bit in big games. I usually like to beat them up the middle, and beat them in places they don't think you are going to hit them.

What gave me most pleasure was doing the right things at the right times, and doing what other teams did not think we were going to do.

As the fourth season at Central Park came to its end, so the Monie era came to an end. He was on his way to Auckland to coach the Warriors. Little did he know that destiny and the English game had not yet finished with him. There were to be more big games to win.

6

AUCKLAND WARRIORS CALL

'If tombstones could talk and tell the truth,
everyone would want to be buried at sea!'

When Maurice Lindsay, the Wigan chairman, made it known that he wished to be considered for the job of chief executive of the Rugby League, replacing the retiring David Oxley, the die was cast for Monie. He realised that the club had gone as far as it could. In his opinion, once Lindsay left, there would be an inevitable slide. The drive, energy, enthusiasm and, most importantly, the rugby acumen would leave with the chairman. John Monie has made no secret of the fact that he considered Lindsay to be one of the best administrators in the game. Also, he realised there is never a good time to leave a successful club, but if Lindsay was to go he would go also.

It was somewhat ironic then that it should be his own chairman who talked him into staying on at Central Park when really he wished to leave. As he said:

> I was not really bothered about it while Maurice was in charge, simply because I had as much faith in him as he had in me. He was rugby league through and through, just

> as I am. Originally when I moved over from Parramatta I had signed to stay at Wigan for two years. Maurice convinced me to stay a third year. As everyone in the game will tell you, he could be very persuasive if he wanted something. He pointed out that I knew just what Jack Robinson, the incoming chairman, was like, and if I could give the club one more year, it would help Jack through. Maurice felt that it was too much for the club, to lose its chairman and coach at the same time, too unsettling. The club had always prided itself on its stable administration. Maurice didn't want to see it all crumble.

It was not to be long before Monie was to see first hand the differing approach of the new man! Gone was Lindsay the innovator, the thinker, the gambler. Robinson was from a different mould entirely – a conservative antique dealer.

Monie was back in Australia on his close-season holiday. While there, he was negotiating with the great Aussie centre Gene Miles to return to Wigan for a second season.

> Gene had had a great season and I was keen to get him back. I was delighted when we agreed a deal. I rang the chairman [Jack Robinson] and he was not interested. He told me he had signed a replacement who was a lot cheaper! The replacement was Andrew Farrar: a tough, uncompromising, talented player. Andrew could not do the things Gene could but he did prove to be a good signing for the club. At the end of the season Jack did not re-sign Farrar in spite of his great contribution and his desire to come back. It was not good business. It was the same with Andy Gregory, the scrum-half. Jack sold him to Leeds and brought in a reserve-grade half-back from Warrington. That was the difference between Jack and Maurice, who would only bring in a player if he was better than the ones we had. Jack was happy to bring in lesser players because they

> cost less. I think a lot of the problems were caused by the fact that Jack was not really a good judge of players, but he thought he was.

In spite of such setbacks, Monie was not a man to brood and take his ball home.

> It has always been my philosophy that, as a coach, I have to work with the players I have got, rather than the ones I would like to have, or did have and had lost. With Gene, he was such an exciting player that people would come through the turnstiles just to watch him; he could do so much with the ball in hand, he just gave a club so much. To be fair to Andrew Farrar, that season he was at the club he was probably the best centre in England, in my opinion. He was different from Miles, much more defensive, but he had a great season. However, you see the difference between Maurice and Jack right there. Maurice had this philosophy that when you went shopping you always bought off the top shelf. Jack on the other hand, well, Jack always looked for the cheaper buy. He struck lucky with one of his buys, though, which was Frano Botica. Jack used up one of the import spots at the club with an untried union man. To accommodate Frano, Jack cut Steve Hampson, who really had done nothing wrong. 'Hampo' was denied a testimonial year at a time when he had plenty of football left in him!

During that year the club knew that it was to be Monie's last with them and once the news leaked out it sparked off interest down under. It surprised many people in the game that Robinson appeared to make little effort to persuade Monie to stay a bit longer; perhaps he knew such an approach would be futile. Equally surprising was that he made no move to get a replacement in place before Monie actually stepped down! John

Monie, though, found himself in demand, and especially down under, which pleased him enormously.

He was particularly attractive to the soon-to-be-formed expansion clubs in the Australian Winfield Cup competition. They saw in him a world-class coach who would give credibility to their efforts to produce a club which could compete in what is, after all, the toughest arena in the rugby league world. Equally, they were getting a coach who would attract sponsorship and sponsors, an ever-increasing persona, given the way the game was and is moving, a coach who was media friendly, who could get the press 'on side', as it were. Finally, they were getting a coach who was well liked and respected within the game on both sides of the world, who could attract players to a club. It showed that the administration was taking the task seriously and wanted to be competitive.

Laurie Puddie, the chairman of the newly formed Perth Western Reds in Western Australia, flew over to England and had talks with Monie. He must have felt the man had what was needed to front his new outfit. A deal was tentatively agreed between the two. Puddie went back home and Monie waited for final details to be hammered out, but nothing happened. Puddie never got back to him. Perhaps the politics of the game in that state were just too much for Puddie to overcome. The Reds actually appointed Peter Mulholland as head coach. He had a successful record in schools rugby and that did not help their cause in bringing the top-notch players to Perth.

However, contact was made by another Laurie, this time Laurie Stubbing at Auckland. Stubbing and Peter McCloud approached Monie with the idea of him coaching New Zealand's first-ever Winfield Cup competition club. As he said:

> When the news first got out I had a number of phone calls from Sydney clubs, so there was interest there. That pleased me because I had been out of the Sydney competition for almost four years. I know we had been successful at Wigan,

> but I did not really know how that would be viewed back home. I was thoroughly impressed with Auckland, and the way they went about doing business, more so than I was with the Reds. I felt the Warriors knew where they were heading. They had done a great deal of ground work before they talked to me. They also had a philosophy, knew what they wanted to achieve in the game, equally when they wanted to achieve it. They wanted to provide a platform for home-grown talent to play the game at the highest level without having to move across the Tasman Sea to do it, as so many had done previously!

It was a challenge that appealed to him. Little did he know that in a very short space of time it was to turn him from Wigan Saint to Wigan Satan! It seemed that soon after he left Central Park, a campaign was orchestrated to discredit him. The local newspaper carried the story that Monie was coming back to poach players from the club. As if that were not bad enough, one of the players he was to take away with him was Dean Bell, the one person who was held so highly in the spectators' esteem that he ranked only marginally below the coach. The supporters saw their club losing two inspirational figures, even if Bell was to complete one more year for Wigan before moving back home, in September 1994. People thought he could play forever but now they could see him leaving the club. Most certainly they, like any supporters, were not happy about the situation.

Things got worse when it became known that Andy Platt, the prop forward, along with his second-row colleague, Dennis Betts, was contemplating joining Monie down under. The newspaper campaign got quite vitriolic with a headline which read, 'Monie is the root of all evil!'

The campaign turned positively apoplectic when the story broke that Frano Botica, Wigan's point-scoring machine, would also be playing for the Warriors. The local paper carried a photograph of Monie on which they had superimposed devil's horns and a tail! It was a campaign that the chairman Jack Robinson seemed happy to fuel, and this against a coach who had delivered the double once more for him before he left.

Monie is much more philosophical about the whole thing now. At the time it hurt him a great deal.

> I suppose Jack was pretty insecure at the time, new to the chairman's job and losing a coach. I think he felt that he had to be seen to be doing his job in the eyes of the Wigan supporters. I did not agree with the methods he used, but that was Jack!

It must be said that the chairman did have a ready-made scapegoat on which he could vent his spleen. He did so with relish. Robinson had a reputation as being a somewhat fiery character, and it certainly showed at this particular spell in his chairmanship of the Wigan club.

Robinson claimed that Monie had been acting for the Auckland club while he was being paid by Wigan. If that were not bad enough, here he was now, poaching players from the club he had just left. In all probability the players had been approached by Monie while he was still at Central Park so, in Robinson's opinion, adding insult to injury. Robinson gave the impression that it was Monie's intention to transport the whole Wigan team, lock, stock and barrel, down to New Zealand. It was a notion the local newspapers were happy to support; after all, it helped sell papers at a time when the sport was supposedly going through the quiet period of the close season. Nothing could have been further from the truth. After all, the Auckland club, like the three other newcomers and, I suppose, like any other club, had drawn up a list of players they were interested in. This had been carried out well before Monie had been approached or even appointed. There is no doubt that he also added his recommendations to the list. However, even if he had wanted to take the whole Wigan squad, the New Zealand club board would never have agreed to it. In all probability, nor could they afford it. All of this mattered little, logic went out of the window as the campaign against Monie gained momentum.

> While I was at Wigan in that last season, once the deal had been agreed with Auckland, which was actually signed on 16 December 1992, all the media in England were informed of the fact. They were also asked not to broach the New Zealand subject with me. I really did want to get down and concentrate on the job in hand, which was making sure I left the Wigan club on as big a high as I could. Perhaps to go for the double once again or perhaps even the treble! I think a lot of people had no idea of the pressure on both the players and myself to keep winning. The club had experienced the most phenomenal success in the previous three years, and the pressure to maintain that was very high. Not only did the supporters expect it; I felt that a great many in the media, who perhaps should have known better, did too. We were expected to win every match, perform at the top of our game week in and week out. If we did not, then you would see the question being asked, 'Was the Wigan bubble about to burst?' As it turned out, we did the double once again, and I left on the back of another fantastic season.

Monie was saddened by the whole episode, which occurred once he had left, and wanted to set the record straight. He never really got the chance. He actually instigated legal action against the chairman for defamation of character. Monie received many calls and newspaper cuttings informing him of all the accusations; it was as if Jack Robinson and the English media felt that Monie was never going to know, or find out what was being said about him. He did, of course, he was told everything. (Coaches have a very good spy network!) He dropped the case before it got to court. Although he felt he was justified in bringing the court action, Monie thought the publicity would damage the Wigan club more than it would damage the chairman. Also the feeling was that the chairman didn't seem to care a damn anyway, as he would never be convinced that Monie had not acted in an underhand manner. It all went sour, though, for chairman Robinson. Many people believed he lost a great deal of respect and friendship as a result of his criticism of his former coach. While it was not the end of the club's golden era, many believe that it was most certainly the beginning of a cycle which would see the club taken literally to the very edge of extinction. In spite of his efforts to get the truth out into the open, Monie felt people never did get the real story.

As he pointed out to those prepared to listen, who were few in number and many thousands of miles away, Dean Bell fully intended to retire when his contract with Wigan was completed. In fact, Monie knew that the Wigan club had no intention of offering him a new contract when his existing one ended in 1994. Monie, together with his wife Julie, put it to Dean that one more year as captain of the Auckland Warriors would be a perfect way to end his illustrious career. It must be said that this was done in October 1993, some five months after he had completed his Wigan contract. Bell decided to give his coach one more season and agreed to move back to his native land. He also knew that in all probability he would not be offered a new deal by Wigan. Monie was offering him a chance to extend his career by another season, and at the very highest level. He felt that he had that one last season in him and where better to play it than in his home country? He never regretted for one moment his decision to return home for that one season. Had he not done so, in all probability he would have kept to his word and retired from the game while at the very top. Hardly a former coach poaching a player, as the chairman claimed.

The two forwards, Andy Platt and Dennis Betts, were not

actually signed by Monie. Ian Robson, who was the chief executive of the Auckland Warriors at the time, confirmed this. It was the then chief executive of the Warriors, Ian Robson, who in late December 1993 returned to England. While in England, he met and talked to both players and signed them to contracts. Monie may well have wanted them, as he said they would be wanted at the club simply because of the good habits they had acquired.

> Platty was always first at training and last to leave. He never missed a weights session. Betts was the same, both had that attitude you wanted to rub off on the younger players you brought into the club.

Even so, it was Robson who actually got them to sign for the Warriors. It was Robson who convinced them their future was in a new country with a new club, not Monie.

> Andy Platt was actually coming to the end of his contract with the club. I knew that. Also I knew we needed to get some experience into the Warriors, if we were to have any success. The club, though, had more or less done a deal with Ian Roberts, the Aussie test prop, in September, so when I met Andy Platt in October, we had no need for him then.
>
> John and I, in October 1993, went to England for the Kiwis' tour. Monie was actually working for Sky Sport and was also to carry out other guest duties in connection with the Test series. We were staying in a hotel quite close to Buckingham Palace and took Dean Bell, his wife and his good friend Andy Platt out to dinner. I still remember the first time I saw Platty; I thought, this is 'Popeye' in the flesh! I said to John later, 'What's wrong with him? Why don't we sign him?' Unfortunately we had gone a long way

down the path with Ian Roberts, the Aussie Test prop; we had exchanged letters and got a verbal agreement with him. Sadly, we had not got that magic pen onto the contract. While we were on that trip I actually rang Ian and asked, 'You are right, aren't you? If you are not we will be disappointed, but here in England we think we can sign someone else.' He assured me there was no problem. So I did not talk about contracts with Andy.

Unfortunately the deal with Ian fell through in November and we decided to make contact again with Andy. The board agreed to try to sign him instead of Roberts. Not only did I know Andy Platt was coming to the end of his career with Wigan, I also knew we needed to sign a prop who would give us the go forward that Roberts would have done.

It was in December 1993 that I rang Andy to talk to him. He is a straight up and down good bloke and he said to me, 'You were over here two months ago; why did you not talk to me then, what's gone wrong?' As he had been straight with me I was the same with him. I told him that Futon and Stanton at Manly, having got wind of our approach, had basically upped the ante to keep Ian at the club. I told Andy, 'If you think that makes you second choice you deal with it, I am jumping on a plane to come and sign you.'

That is what Robson did. In late December 1993 he returned and had orders to sign a number of players with whom he had been negotiating. Even then it was not without its moments, as he said:

I was the target of the fans' disaffection in Wigan, not John Monie. I think every pub in Wigan had a wanted poster up with my face on it! I slipped into town and on the first night went up to see a friend, Alan, the landlord at the Tudor Inn in Wrightington. I walked in and immediately

> saw John Dorahy, the Wigan coach, having dinner with his family. He knew what I was there for and was not pleased. I was sprung on the first evening! I exchanged pleasantries with him and thought, 'Well, let's see what happens.'

During that trip, Robson managed to sign up Tea Ropati from St Helens, 'Tiny' Solomona from Oldham, and Platt. As he said, though, he had talks with a lot of players: Kevin Iro, Gary Freeman, Jason Mackie, Tawara Nikau, whom he had tracked during the earlier Kiwi tour in October 1993, and one young Wigan player whom they did not sign. However, the meeting provided him with an embarrassing incident a few hours later.

> We had agreed to meet the player and his agent at John Monie's house and talk. I stressed the need for confidentiality so as not to embarrass anyone. We met on the Saturday and the following day Wigan were to play away against Castleford. We had arranged to get tickets, and I think Dean Bell got them. So we turned up just after kick-off at Castleford, with tickets for the Wigan directors' box. We walked up the stairs and turned right to get to our seats. All we got from the directors' box was 'daggers'! No one would talk to us, not even a 'good day'. Dean Bell was not playing, so I turned and asked him what we had done. He asked us if we had read the papers. Apparently there was an article in the press about Monie and Robson in a secret meeting to do a deal with the Wigan star and his agent. It is funny looking back now, but at the time it was very embarrassing.

The player was Barrie-Jon Mather, who at the time was just breaking into Monie's first-team squad. Robson's cover had been blown quite by chance, as he and John Monie were saying their goodbyes to Mather and his agent a local reporter who lived close by drove past. Ironically, Mather was eventually to sign for Perth

Western Reds after a protracted legal battle with the Wigan club. Jack Robinson, along with his half-brother Jim Hartley (both of whom were good friends of the then Reds coach Peter Mulholland), had a big go at him after Mather signed for the Reds outfit. So the truth about the signing of the Wigan players was a fair distance away from Monie poaching Andy Platt, Dean Bell and Frano Botica away from Wigan.

It was a different story with the second-row man Dennis Betts. He was also coming to the end of his current contract with Wigan. Monie explained:

> Dennis expressed a desire to see if he could handle the Sydney competition. That attitude is only natural, I think, at least in any player worth his salt. The top players do want to play the game at the very highest level; Dennis was no exception. When we approached him he was only too pleased to move and give the Aussie comp a go. After all, he had achieved all there was to achieve at Wigan. As I said, he had all the good attitudes I wanted youngsters to acquire and I was delighted when we got him on board at the Warriors.

It was, however, Robson who was again responsible for getting Betts to the Warriors on his visit to England in the December of 1993.

> What John said was true and I used that as the greatest selling point I had with Dennis. I can still remember Dennis coming to see me on an earlier trip and we were keen to sign him then. He and his agent were there and had jotted some figures down on an envelope. We compared what we could afford, given the salary cap down under, the budget we had to work to and the exchange rate at the time, against the shortfall on his existing contract. There was a substantial

gulf. Basically, we walked away saying, 'A great idea, but regrettably we're not in the same ball park.'

It was only on that December trip that I talked with Dennis again. We had been lucky with some of the players we had acquired. It had freed up a little more money for us. Dennis told me Jack Robinson, the Wigan chairman, had told him he was considered one of the foundation stones of the Wigan club. I pointed out that if he were the foundation stone of my club I would not leave him with just a year to run on his contract. Jack knew that there were four expansion clubs coming into the Sydney comp in 1995. Dennis was 23 or 24 and nothing was being done to tie him up, knowing full well that people like me would be knocking at his door. I would not wish to criticise the Wigan chairman; he had to work in his own way. However, I certainly would not have allowed Dennis Betts to get so close to the end of his contract without making moves to tie him up again.

I kept telling Dennis the freakish time he had had at Wigan meant there was not a lot else to achieve in the game in England. Why not come to Australia? You have had a taste of it through international football, now come and truly demonstrate your international credibility as a professional rugby league player by doing it week in and week out, in what is still, today, the toughest rugby league competition in the world!

Betts signed for Robson's Warriors. So while Monie may have made the initial approach, it was Robson's persuasive tongue which got him to make the commitment.

Frano Botica, the last of the Warriors' acquisitions from Wigan, was at the time looking to return to his homeland. He had enjoyed his time at Wigan, breaking all sorts of scoring records during his relatively short time there, but he felt that it was time to go home. What many have forgotten is that while he went to Auckland it was initially only to be on a short-term contract, to play until the season in England started. He did what many players had done before him; he signed a short-term deal, fully intending to return to Wigan before ending his career either at Central Park or having one last season in his own country with Monie. Sadly, even that was not to be. He broke a leg playing against, strangely enough, the Western Reds of Perth, so he returned to Wigan injured. A short time later he was transferred by the chairman to Castleford. He had, though, been honest with his coach while at the Warriors, telling him that the level of competition was too much for him at that time in his career.

Yet again it was Robson who actually got Botica to sign on the dotted line. 'I signed up Frano at the Holiday Inn in Leeds when he was "cooking bones", barbecuing one evening during the tour.' As Monie argued, it was hardly the work of a man trying to poach a whole squad of players. The actual truth was that it was only four players, two of whom were coming to the end of their career and the club would not be re-signing, and from the forwards only Betts had actually been targeted – this from a squad which had won the cup and league double four times during his reign: a squad of nearly thirty players and a reserve-grade squad which had also swept all before it. It must have seemed strange to Monie to hear the outpourings about poaching after all he had witnessed on the other side of the coin while at Wigan. When it became known that Martin Offiah was unsettled at Widnes, Monie watched the club pursue him with a ruthless determination. Wigan were up there with the best when it came to poaching players from other clubs.

It must also be said, in Monie's defence, that the club in its first season after his departure once again completed a cup and league double under new coach John Dorahy. However, Dorahy's reward from chairman Robinson was 'the sack'. Immediately after the cup-final triumph at Wembley against Leeds, he was dismissed and Graeme West appointed in a 'caretaker' capacity until the end of the season. Even then, the club managed to win the premiership, then travelled to Brisbane to meet the Broncos in the World Club Championship.

In Brisbane, against all the odds, they pulled off arguably the greatest win in the club's history, to be crowned World Club Champions. It has been forgotten that they did so without the services of centre and skipper Dean Bell or prop Andy Platt. Ironically, Monie was guest speaker at a function after the game, as well as commentating for television on the game itself. Many people in England felt that even though he was no longer at the club, it was 'his' team that had triumphed.

> It was good to see them win; I felt that when I left the club it was in better shape than at any time in its history. It showed on the night; they still knew how to win big games. It was a habit which had been worked on during the four years I had been at Wigan. I had coached at Parramatta when they had won everything in the same season. I had also done the same at Wigan when the first, reserve and academy grades had all won the cup and the league championship. I don't think they were going to miss four players somehow! Whatever damage I may or may not have done did not put the club into the hole they were to find themselves in a few years down the track.

Monie had an enjoyable evening following the game, not only because of the win, but also because of the reunion he had with the players and with Graeme West, who had been his reserve-grade coach at Wigan. He even found time to shake the hand of chairman Robinson.

> I met up with Jack. To be fair, he was always pleasant enough face to face. I congratulated him on the win and he

was okay with me. As I said, I felt he thought he had to stir the pot, as it were. Mind you, he was a little erratic at times. He did at one time have arguably the two best wing men in the world in Martin Offiah and Jason Robinson, and still went out and bought 'Inga the Winga' Tuigamala! Again an untried rugby union convert using up an import spot – a player who had spent more time on the reserve bench than on the field the previous season.

The actual leaving of Wigan and joining Auckland pales into insignificance compared to the trauma created by the chairman and the local newspaper. However, as was stated earlier, it was the phone calls from Laurie Stubbing and Peter McLeod that were to take Monie to the other side of the world. Having decided to make the move to New Zealand, Monie, along with Ian Robson, set about the task of building a squad of players from scratch.

I knew we had to get some experience from Australia into the club – players who knew the Winfield Cup. We needed to instil good work and training habits and we did not have the time to wait for that to happen. We brought in the experience from England in the shape of Dean Bell, who was a fantastic captain in that first season for us, and Andy Platt who was just a great inspiration to all around him, although we did have a problem with his knee initially.

When Andy arrived, we sent him to see a specialist to basically clean up the wear and tear in his knee. To put it bluntly, the surgeon did not do a good job, and for a couple of months after the operation Andy was running around as if he had a wooden leg. It looked at one stage as if he would never play again! So I don't think we got the best out of him on the field, through no fault of his own. We brought in Betts and Botica for their experience, along with Duane Mann, the hooker from Warrington. Duane at the time was the New Zealand Test hooker. Also we got Tea Ropati, the

> Saints stand-off or centre, who was in the Test team along with Duane.
>
> From Australia we brought in Greg Alexander and Phil Blake. In keeping with the philosophy at the club, we also brought in some outstanding Kiwi players: Stephen Kearney, Syd Eru, Gene Ngamu and Stacy Jones, who had all made a big impression as Junior Kiwis.

It was testimony to Stacy Jones' ability that Monie eventually moved Greg Alexander to full-back in order that he might play Jones at half-back. This was at a time when Jones was only an eighteen year old and Greg was considered to be a world-class half-back! With the experience from three countries, coupled with the best of the young, home-grown talent, the Warriors built a very competitive club.

It was not all plain sailing, however. As was mentioned earlier, Ian Roberts slipped through the Warriors' net and there was another spectacular slip-up! Henry Paul, an outstanding Junior Kiwi, was allowed to leave the club and move to Wigan – strange that Jack Robinson did not complain about that deal. Wigan made Henry an offer fifteen times the amount we had offered to younger players.

The club had also signed Kiwi centre Ruben Wiki from the Canberra Raiders. When it became known, the Raiders spat the dummy out, claiming they had an option on him. Surprisingly, it took Canberra quite a while to get round to spitting it out. When the Warriors signed Wiki, he was not playing particularly outstanding football, and was in reserve grade. As luck would have it, though, with the season drawing to a close, Wiki was in superb form. He put together a number of stand-out performances as the business end of the season approached. So much so that it had prompted the Raiders to offer him a new deal, a deal which topped the one he had signed for the Warriors. He, not surprisingly, in turn claimed he wished to stay with the Raiders. When the whole sorry business came before the authorities it was decided that Wiki was to stay with the Raiders. One reason for the decision given by the court was that Monie had been in the room with Wiki when he had signed the Auckland contract and that, it was deemed, had placed undue pressure on the player to sign. While the Aussies might well want to expand the competition, there was no way they were going to go out of their way, to the extent of supporting a New Zealand club over an Aussie one – God forbid!

Robson considered that incident with Wiki to be personally and professionally the lowest point and greatest disappointment of his time at the Warriors.

> We actually settled the case on advice. It had become apparent that from the nature of the evidence they were tabling and the apparent sympathy from the judge that we were on a hiding to nothing. One argument put forward was that having John Monie around both in the negotiation process and particularly at the time Wiki signed the contract was intimidating, given his limited education. This claim we rejected outright as we had a number of meetings with him. We had seen him play and talked to him on previous occasions. We knew he was a hidden jewel down there in the Canberra reserve grade. He was a player I feel we lost because we were not bold enough. We had a budget and could not afford to risk signing too many young players who may or may not produce the goods. Certainly Ruben never looked back after that court case!

The irony of the situation was that the son of the presiding judge in the case, David Gallup, is now the legal adviser to the National Rugby League (NRL) and a very good mate of Ian Robson!

The weeks and months leading up to the initial entry into the Winfield Cup competition were exciting times for Monie.

There is more to winning a footy game than the eighty minutes on game day. It is what you do in the week leading up to the game which is important. In that respect the experienced players we had were superb. They taught the younger players how to prepare for a match, how to look after themselves, what to eat, when to sleep. They were really magnificent. One player we brought into the club never really got the credit he deserved. That was John Kerwin, the ex-All Black. He was not in the original squad of players we signed, but he brought so much to the club.

He had done it all in rugby union. He knew how to prepare when travelling to an away game, and people forget that every other week we were travelling over one thousand miles [1,500 km] to play away matches. That amount of travelling really can take it out of you. Kerwin was used to winning, and winning away from home. It was a habit with him and he passed on so much of that attitude to the club. As I said, he never really got the credit he deserved.

I also felt the club never got the credit it deserved in New Zealand for finishing tenth out of twenty after that first season. That, I think, was mainly due to the media. You have to realise that the whole country was used to the All Blacks travelling over to Australia or South Africa and coming away with a win, in fact expecting to win. There was always a massive outcry in the country were the All Blacks to lose a match or not play particularly well. They could not, or would not, realise that in rugby league the boot was on the other foot. It was the Australians who were the better players, it was they who came over to New Zealand or England expecting to win. No, I think the club had a great first season, even though the media were always quick to criticise the club, simply because of the union mentality. They could not get their heads around the notion that at league the Kiwis were second

> best to the Australians; it irked them. Why could we not win every game? After all, the All Blacks did!

It is a viewpoint that has the full support of his then chief executive Ian Robson.

> There were some silly things said but I refuse to let them diminish my positive memories of the four years I was with the Warriors. Our nearest away game was a three-hour journey by plane. The Super Twelve comp in rugby union is an eleven-week competition; ours was a thirty-week season. We did it in that '95 season with a bunch of guys who had never done anything like it before. We finished tenth, but all people remember is that in the last three games we got terrible hidings. We did fall into a hole towards the end. That first season was a few weeks too far for us. Saying that, if results had gone our way in the last round of the competition we would have made the play-off stage, which would have been an unbelievable performance.

It was not to be, but the lead-up to that first season and the season itself was a tremendous experience for Monie.

7

MONIE THE KIWI

'Criticism can strengthen or weaken you. If you have good character it will make you stronger. If you have poor character it will make you weaker!'

Monie left Wigan at the end of the 1993–94 season and had over a year to prepare for his next competitive game, which would be in charge of the new Auckland Warriors. He had, by his own admission, been compiling a 'hit list' of players he would like to see at the new club. The odd thing was that until he went to New Zealand he had never even spoken to Ian Robson, the chief executive! Monie's wife Julie had spoken more to Robson than he had. It just seemed that each time Robson rang Monie in Wigan he was at training. Monie arrived in New Zealand to meet with Robson for the first time. Never having met Monie, Robson did not want to do so for the first time under the spotlight of intense media coverage. Robson arranged security clearance from immigration for himself, and met Monie as he stepped off the airplane and before he and Julie had cleared customs. Monie jokingly said, as they shook hands for the first time, 'So, you're the guy who has been having an affair over the phone with my wife!' This somewhat bizarre first meeting had not stopped the recruitment campaign from getting under way.

I sat down with Ian in Auckland and went through a whole list of players who were available. Right from day one our philosophy at Auckland was going to be that we would give young New Zealand players the opportunity to stay in the country and play for the Warriors. The plan was that after four or five seasons we would be able to bring the best of the local junior players through.

When I got to Auckland one of the first things I did was to go to the under-18 championships. There, we signed up a few of the better players; Henry Paul was one, and others we signed up were Brian Henare, Joe Vegana and Brady Malem. While we had some of the best youngsters in the country, we also had senior players in our sights. Any players who had gone to Sydney were targeted – Stephen Kearney among them! So the second part of our plan was to hit on all the New Zealand players who were playing out of the country. Before I left England we spoke to Solamona, Nikau, Blackmore and others to see if they were interested.

We wanted to bring all the senior players back that we could. Then we looked at an Australian half-back, Greg Alexander. We had a very good half-back at the club in Stacy Jones, but he was only around seventeen at the time. In our first season I was not about to go into the Sydney competition with Stacy at his age.

So it was that Monie and Robson assembled a squad of players that would make up the first- and reserve-grade teams for the new outfit. That done, it was Monie's job to mould them into a team which would be able to compete well in the toughest competition in the world. He had a clear idea in his mind what was needed from his players.

I was already familiar with the way they played in Sydney, even when at Wigan I kept a close eye on what they were doing there. To be successful required firstly a lot of talent in the side, then a pair of good half-backs. You needed a strong front row, so all your front-row players had to be like back-row players, your back-row players like centres, but none had to sacrifice size! We were looking for penetration in the centres, a good captain, which I was confident we had in Dean Bell, and a little bit of extra, that players like Phil Blake provided. He was a player who was a bit different from the run-of-the-mill player; he could do something off the cuff which would break a tight game. Greg Alexander was another with that extra quality as well.

Monie was used to the pressure that comes from running a club, and the pressure that supporters and club chairmen put on a coach. At Auckland he certainly had that. He also had the weight of expectation of the whole of New Zealand, but did not succumb to this added weight of a nation whose eyes were on him.

In the beginning I was not sure whether they were taking us seriously or not! The All Blacks were on top of the world at the time. Union was very strong in Auckland; it was the centre of their power. Many of the Auckland Blues were All Blacks and the skipper Shaun Fitzpatrick was from Auckland. All the press in New Zealand, and particularly in Auckland, was geared towards the All Blacks. I think the rugby league writers were guys who were not good enough to write about rugby union. Union attracted the biggest sponsors; people were falling over themselves to sponsor that game. We were the new kids on the block.

New kids they may have been, but the Australian rugby league authorities did them no favours. Their first-ever match was to be against the Brisbane Broncos, at home in the Erikson stadium. Brisbane were, at that time, the champions, so it was a big test for Monie's new charges. Both he and they were ready for it!

We opened up with a game against Brisbane. The rugby league hierarchy chartered a jumbo and flew themselves and all the rugby league journalists to all four games involving the new expansion clubs: Perth, Adelaide, Townsville, and then over to Auckland, to take in all four games. For us it was just a huge night; I think we had over thirty thousand crammed into the stadium for the game. We were actually winning the ball game twenty-five minutes or so into the second half, then up popped Alfie Langer, who put a step on Tiny Solomona to score by the posts, and that was the game gone.

I was pleased with our performance in that first game. The players, I think, were perhaps relieved that they had put on a great show against Brisbane. Naturally, they were disappointed they had lost the game, but I think mostly everyone was relieved that all the hard work, the effort of pre-season training was all over and we were actually in competition. We were all looking forward to getting our teeth into it.

The reaction of the home press was good to see. I thought that night they sat up and started to take notice of us. It became obvious that we were going to be more than just novelty value to them. They realised that we were going to be a major sporting attraction out of Auckland. I do not think the All Blacks saw it as a threat, which was something I agreed with. I have always believed that in top-line sport there is room for everybody from the different codes. As it turned out, that season we were able to play in front of crowds of twenty-six or twenty-seven thousand people in our home games. It was a crowd many of the Sydney sides would have welcomed!

John Monie's Diary

Monie was both an avid reader and diarist as this section from his 1997 diary shows.

APRIL 1997

DESIRE

Sometimes desire is more important than talent or even a healthy body.

How good do you want to be?

A coach can guide you, instruct you, give you direction. But you must do the rest.

This desire must come from within, not from your coaches. It must come from you long before you run out for the game. That's why training is so important. It builds desire long before the match starts.

JULY 1997

TEAMWORK

It's great that you have individual talent; you will get plenty of opportunities to use it, but teamwork wins it.

Everybody do something, play for the team – that's what is important. Did the team win? Did I contribute? Who do we play next?

If that first game at Erikson stadium caused organisational problems for the club, the following match away from home was to set the tone for problems the club would always face – being based in New Zealand. An away trip was uncharted territory, not only for Monie, but also for the players. They had played 'on the road' before but only in friendly games. Now it was for real. People expected success, the press expected success, and the club expected success.

We tried to treat it just like any other game, but as we were to learn throughout the season, one of the most difficult obstacles for any team is living in a different time zone. We

> faced a three-and-a-half-hour flight, minimum, to play our away games. That was just the time of the flight, but we also had the time difference between Auckland and Sydney. We had to get to the airport, making sure the guys were there early enough, load all the gear onto the coach, then off the coach and onto the aircraft, and then repeat the operation once we had arrived in Sydney. There were delays caused by waiting to take off, or in unloading at the other end. Finally, when you added it all up, it could be a long day by the time you got to the team hotel. Last of all, you had the problem that it would be 8.00 p.m. in Sydney but it was really 10.00 p.m. in Auckland. It was much more complicated than just a three-and-a-half-hour flight!

One of the other expansion clubs had a similar problem. The Perth Western Reds club faced a five-hour flight to Sydney every other week to play their away fixture. Airplane food was not really suitable for rugby league players, simply because there was not enough of it. They, in fact, made arrangements with the airline Ansett, who incidentally were also one of the club's sponsors, for rugby-player-sized portions to be supplied in flight to the players. It was not a problem the Auckland Warriors met; in fact, the reverse was more the case.

> A lot of the team were Polynesians; we had a very big side and, if anything, I thought we actually ate too much when we got to Australia. We would have a buffet-style evening meal, and the players got up the next morning to another big buffet-type breakfast. You would have players taking food back to their room, as happens anywhere. In a way I thought our players were probably overeating. The food on the plane was a minor consideration for me. Early in our life we made a conscious decision that whenever we played away and it was an afternoon kick-off, we would do everything in our power to get on the last flight to Auckland. If there was any

chance at all of getting that last plane we would do it. Sometimes it meant players walking into a shower and almost straight out again at the other side. Helpers had all the gear packed and loaded on the coach outside the changing-rooms. We would virtually run straight off the field, to the showers, onto the coach and were gone! The thinking behind it was to get everyone home as quickly as possible and spend the next day assessing injuries, having a team meeting, breaking down the game from the video and getting the players to exercise either by running or in the pool. Our game plan was always to get over to Sydney the day before the game and do everything possible to get on that plane home on game day.

For the opposition it was a 'novelty'; after all they only faced the journey once. The travel problems were something Monie knew the club would have to live with if they were to be successful.

I have to admit we found the travel hard in the second and third season, and it became particularly hard to win games in Sydney at night. Perth, I suppose, was the extreme case, because by the time we had kicked off in Perth it was midnight in Auckland! The time delay certainly affected the team in the second half of games. When they said to me the team had faded a little in the second half, I used to say to a few of the journalists in Auckland, 'Well, what are you doing around eleven or twelve o'clock at night?'

That first season had many high spots for Monie, but in typical modest fashion his comment was that just being back in the Sydney competition was the highest point for him.

I was really pleased we had recruited well; we were not whipping boys for anybody, we were competitive. Because of the make-up of our team we lost a few games in the last

> twenty minutes; I see the club still doing it now. We were true to the policy we had set out with: not having too many Australians, and setting up a pathway for the younger players to come through into the first grade. We were still competitive.

Monie and Robson recruited players who had the qualities they were looking for, so that each would add a little extra to the club. They were tried and tested professionals but an unknown quantity was how the younger players would fare in the heat of battle, week in and week out. There were some successes even in that early first season in the club's history, which gave Monie great pleasure.

> Stacy Jones was one 'bolter', so by the end of the season I had to move Greg Alexander to full-back to fit Jones into the side. He was one who, regardless of his age, said, 'Hey, I am ready to play first grade.' That was a real bonus for us; we had never even dreamed that we could take one of the youngest players in our two squads and throw him into first grade. Joe Vagana also had a fair taste of it in first grade, Willie Poching was always thereabouts, and Martin Moana was another.
>
> There were blunders as well in that first season. I actually put an extra substitute on during one game! We won the game easily – 36–8 – so it was not even close. I asked a couple of people who worked for us to go and check with the fourth official on the side line about how many subs I had used. The word came back we could make one more substitution, so I brought Joe Vagana off and put Willie Poching on for the last five minutes to give him a little experience against a Sydney side. It was not even a tight game and I did not need to do it. A woman journalist from New Zealand rang the Australian Rugby League to ask them to check the number of subs we had used because she thought we had used one too many. For the first training

session after that game I rolled up a big Warriors' poster into a dunce's cap, put it on, and walked into training. That broke the guys up straightaway; everyone had a bit of a laugh. Then I took it off and said, 'That's the end of it; let's get on with the job.'

I think we got on with it well. We finished tenth out of twenty, we beat the other three new clubs in both games to finish ahead of them. That was a better start than Canberra made when they came into the comp. I don't think anyone has ever questioned the amount of talent there was in New Zealand. Our season was always going to depend on how quickly we could adapt to the intensity of the Sydney game, and play week after week at that level of intensity. That was the toughest part of it! They had to front up every week.

We missed Andy Platt for the first couple of months, as was mentioned earlier. Pre-season, he had had surgery on his knee to clean it up, without much success. Our physio had some contacts at North Sydney, having been physio there before marrying a Kiwi and moving to Auckland. Their surgeon cleaned it up the way it should have been done. He sent Platty back with a video of the operation, so we all sat around and looked at all the muck which was cleaned out of his knee and the bits which had been carved up and sucked out.

We had recruited Dennis Betts for his will to win and his attitude. He knew how to go about preparing to win, as did John Kerwin. As it turned out John was our top try-scorer that second season. All of this was passed on to the younger players; this mental toughness and mental preparation to win. It all helped us to succeed that first year. Stephen Kearney was a similar type of player and he had returned from Sydney. Whilst we just missed the play-offs, I think everyone connected with the club felt that it was a job well done. The press thought we had underachieved a little, but

> I think that was because at the time the All Blacks were on top of the world.

The Cinderella first season was completed and preparations made for the second-season assault on the Sydney comp. John Kerwin, the All Black wing legend, had been brought into the club. Things were looking good when the whole rugby league world was hit by the most cataclysmic event in its history. The Murdoch millions were used to introduce 'Super League' to the world. In the UK the concept was eagerly grasped, helped somewhat by £87 million over five years. In Australia the Australian Rugby League were not so welcoming; in fact, Ken Arthurson was positively anti-Super League, arguing that the existing governing body should retain control of the game. The situation in Auckland was that, as the only club, the Warriors had to decide whether they stuck with the ARL or they joined in with the Super League concept. Monie recalled events:

> That was when the whole of Australian Rugby League was hit by the biggest bombshell that it had ever seen. It was a situation which will never happen again. It split friendships, it split the competition. I thought it was a tragedy, really. There was a guy on the board at Auckland named Roger Douglas, who had been the finance minister for New Zealand. Ian, Sir Roger Douglas and myself set up our first meeting with representatives from Super League; it really was all cloak-and-dagger stuff. We met in a hotel in Auckland and, as they say, the rest was history. If we wanted the Auckland Warriors to survive, then we had to accept the News Corporation/limited side of things, which was what we did.
>
> That decision actually split the Warriors' board in half as well. We ended up with board meetings from which details were being taken back to the respective opposition camps. It was just a very, very tough time. In fact, one of the club's

major sponsors, DB Brewery, were initially supportive of the Super League concept. However, once the decision had been finalised, they went 'dirty' on the deal and came out in favour of the ARL! We made a decision from the management side of things at the club about the way we thought things should go. We then got all of our players together and set up a meeting with John Ribot. (The meeting was actually held at my house.) We let the players decide what they wanted, all of them seeing Ribot individually. I had put all the players into three groups, not based on money but based on ability. They spoke to Ribot individually, as I said, and then we asked for their decision. Guys who were on New Zealand $15,000–$20,000 went to Australian $100,000!

Whether the decision was right or wrong, the club survived, and when the competition merged, when the war was over, the club was still in there, in the top competition. They survived; a lot of clubs did not. Adelaide and Perth did not survive, the Mariners in Newcastle did not survive, nor did the Crushers.

On the paddock I think the club stayed the same; we did not improve, we did not kick up. We stayed at the level we had reached in that first year, we were holding on but holding on in a new competition, the Super League. It was a very tough year for us, but in a way we were away from the warring factions. Australia was split down the middle but New Zealand was all Super League, as was England. So we only picked up on the nastiness of what was happening when we went to Australia once every two weeks or so. In the press we had New Zealand journalists who were for the ARL and others who were for Super League; it was a no-win situation. Also the rugby union All Blacks were still on top of the world. So that second season was a tough one for us both on and off the field.

Monie's third season with the club was to prove to be his last. The sad thing from his point of view was that he felt it would be the season which saw the club make that step up to the next level, a level which would see them getting closer to the Sydney teams above them. As is always the case, results take precedence over common sense and patience. Monie saw little of either as that third season began.

> The third season could have been very exciting simply because one of the big Super League signings was Matthew Ridge, who was coming over to Auckland. I personally saw that as a positive. I thought Ridge was the type of player who could take the Warriors from just outside the play-offs and captain them into the finals. He had come out of the Manly club, which had won the competition and had a proven track record. Also, I felt we had never really replaced Dean Bell as captain. Stephen Kearney would have been the perfect captain but he did not want to do it; he felt he was too young to do the job. With Matthew Ridge coming in, I felt he would be the on-field leader that the team so desperately needed. I thought they needed someone who would dominate, who would be very forceful with his ideas. So, in training, I handed a lot of the stuff over to Matthew, so he could become that dominant personality who would captain the side. To some of the outsiders in the early part of that season, it looked as if he was taking over, but it was a conscious decision on the part of myself and the coaching panel. I would be the off-field leader. The difference between the Australian clubs and the Auckland Warriors was that we lacked a leader. I think the guys in New Zealand needed a strong personality whom they could follow.
>
> That season we did have it really tough. The Super League competition was very good; it was a step up for us. Instead of twenty teams there were fourteen, and they were

all good sides. We had moved up a class. We had a tough draw to start the season off and we lost early games. Also, for the guys who had been with us since day one the travelling had become a chore! It was hard, very hard work to get on that aircraft. I let Ridge do a lot of the stuff in training, and some of the journalists in New Zealand who were connected with the ARL competition were very critical of the amount of work and the direction Ridge was taking on the training paddock.

When the end came, it was a shock. It is always a shock. It's hard to handle. You are never prepared for it. But it was a bit of a relief as well. Ian Robson had been sacked earlier in the season, and his last words to me were, 'You will be next, Monie!' There was a real campaign going by this time, claiming that Australians shouldn't be running the Auckland Warriors, that New Zealanders should be running the show. Then, when we got a few bad results, events snowballed. The recipe was always there for disaster.

I had a very good relationship with Ian Robson, but once they put the new chief executive in, who was actually the former chief executive of Soccer New Zealand, which tells you a lot about matters at the club, relations were not the same. I had private meetings with the chief executive, and there must have been private board meetings. In the end he got me. It came in Townsville, actually. We played there and Brian Henare dropped a pass which would have won the game for us. But that game was the last one.

They knew I had been sacked in New Zealand before I did because I remember at the airport the journalists and TV cameras were there. The chief executive was doing a good job keeping them all away from me and sent me down to a private lounge. I was forewarned and, looking back, I knew what was coming.

It was a hard thing for Monie to handle, as he had been in the game at the highest level for fifteen years or more. He had built himself and his family a lovely house at Titirangi in the mountains overlooking the bay at Auckland. It became his refuge for a month or so after the parting of the ways. However, if he thought his days as a coach were ended he was again mistaken because the phone rang.

It was a call from John Martin, who was acting on behalf of Dave Whelan, telling him in a roundabout sort of way that the Wigan club had not done too well in the last couple of seasons. As Monie had predicted, the club had again won the double and the World Club Championship the year he had left. Then the wheels had come off. The new Whitbread stand which had been commissioned in Lindsay's time had gone way over budget. The club was in deep financial crisis; bankruptcy was a real possibility. Dave Whelan was trying to take over the club by buying all the shares off Jack Robinson, the chairman, who was resisting. If Martin and Whelan were successful, would Monie be interested in going back? It was a prospect that whetted his appetite.

> The fact was I had been sacked from Auckland, when I thought I had done a good job. We had a plan in place and we had not deviated too much from it. We were setting the club up to be a New Zealand club, to allow local talent to stay, so I felt a little hard done by. So an opportunity to go back to Wigan from where I had wonderful memories, regardless of Jack Robinson, was good. If there was new management in there and the top people wanted me, I would want to give it a go.
>
> Looking back now at the Auckland club, Frank Endicott took over when I left but the most successful years the club had were still year one and year two. Also, I think they have never had as many top-quality New Zealanders in their squad as they had during those two years. I said to them at the time, 'You are not patient enough; this place will turn

out to be a fantastic franchise.' We had a tough time starting that third season, but you ride through those difficulties, and if you have everyone pulling in the same direction it is a test of character, but the wheel always turns. They were not patient enough. There were different factions in the club who, for whatever reason, wanted upheaval.

It is an old adage that as one door closes, another opens, and Monie had to sit back and watch events unfold twelve and a half thousand miles away in Wigan as Dave Whelan tried to wrestle control of the Wigan club from Jack Robinson.

The club was heading for bankruptcy under Robinson's direction. Allegations of shady transfer dealings involving a Wigan player led to Robinson appearing in court on charges of attempting to pervert the course of justice, although he was cleared of these. The club appeared in the newspapers for the wrong reasons, which was not the Wigan style.

Whelan won the battle, and a few phone calls later the Monie family were on a plane heading back to the scene of some of John's greatest successes.

John Monie's Diary

Monie's diary entry just after being sacked by the Auckland Warriors. May 1997

The bottom line is success and results. The public don't care unless you're winning. They might say once in a while you played well but were unlucky.

If you lose three or four in a row, things soon change. Your past record counts for nothing. It doesn't matter who you are; you are under pressure.

You are dependent on the strength of your board. The strength of their convictions and morals – will they stick with you? They can handle you being criticised, but if the criticism turns to them for employing you, then you are on thin ice.

8

THE PRODIGAL SON RETURNS

'We have earned the right to be called champions in 1999 but we are not just defending the cup! We must go out every week and win it again!'

As Monie had found out, being unemployed is not a happy situation at the best of times. When unemployment is forced upon you, in circumstances over which you have no control, it is downright unpleasant. Therefore, it was with expectation and not a little relief that Monie boarded the flight to England, to take up the reins again at Wigan. In the back of his mind were the thoughts, 'What can be done at the club?' 'What are the underlying reasons leading to the club being unsuccessful on the field?'

It was certainly a club that had changed since his departure; equally the competition in England had changed. The war that had ravaged Australia between the ARL and Super League had not been experienced in the UK. On the contrary, Super League, once the initial shock had subsided, had been welcomed by most clubs. To be more precise, the money on offer had been welcomed by the game in general. The question in Monie's mind was whether the money had had any influence in raising the standard of the game in England.

Certainly the domination his Wigan sides had enjoyed was no longer there. The switch from winter to summer rugby had produced teething troubles for some clubs, including Wigan. Crowds were down, but it was difficult to pinpoint why. Certainly there was a backlash from fans protesting at the way the club was being administered; they were staying away rather than, as they saw it, putting money in the chairman's pocket. The team was not performing well on the paddock and some of the notoriously fickle fans had drifted away. Equally, the switch to summer had alienated others. These were problems that needed to be addressed if the club was to be turned around.

When he arrived at the club he found the problems were much more deep-rooted than even he had thought.

> The place was in a mess. My first impressions on arrival were that a lot of the discipline had gone from the club. The players were certainly not working as hard and were not as focused on the tasks in hand, as shown by little things like telephones going off when you were talking to people. Younger players were walking around the club without much direction; they appeared to be there just for the sake of it.
>
> It was like starting from scratch again. One of the first notes I made was to Marty Hulme, the conditioner I brought with me from Auckland. He was to set up a game between the players, with a ref, just so he and I could take a look at the forty-plus players we had on the books. I knew for sure that we did not need forty players in our first-grade squad. Also, I needed to see how some of them played under a bit of pressure.
>
> When I arrived there were already a number of trials organised: one was against Bradford, another against Saints. I cancelled both of them simply because I did not want to see the players under 'that' sort of pressure. I also

had a problem with Andy Farrell, who I knew was going to be my skipper. I had to check if he needed an arthroscope on a knee which was giving him problems when I arrived. Nothing had been done about it. But the major problem was an apparent breakdown in discipline. Once that goes out of a club you do have problems. There was not a lot of respect there for people and I knew there had been internal upheaval at the club throughout the year. There had also been a lot of bad publicity; people connected with the place had had court cases. Dave Whelan's takeover had at times become a little bit ugly, and there were all kinds of underlying difficulties.

When we arrived, Marty and I looked at each other, had a bit of a smile and I said, 'There's a lot of work to do here, mate! We are going to have to work hard without a break for the next two months!' Training is a good way to begin instilling discipline into a club, simply because it is the first avenue you have open to you which allows you to begin to stamp your presence on the place. There was no hiding place for the players. One of the first things we did was to set up a meeting with them giving them all diaries for the season, along with details of my expectations and a code of conduct for on and off the field, and for match days. I remember one of the rules was simply 'No mobile phones to be taken into the weights room or to be switched on in training time.' Then I asked the players for their expectations on and off the field and on match days. I got them to elect three or four guys to act as spokesmen for the team.

That done, I had to organise video equipment, and make arrangements for food after training sessions, kit out the coaches' room and a players' room with TV and video facilities. I even had to see the chief executive Philip Clarke about Andrew Pinkerton, a masseur who had been at the club a long time. I wanted to get him working a little bit more for us. My major concern, though, apart from these smaller details, was that my squad was over forty strong.

Strange as it seems, even with such a large squad, I realised I needed to bring players in! I also knew that if I brought in Australians, then I needed players who had a great attitude and great work habits. These were the areas I had identified as being lacking at the club. The good work habits were missing, not from the likes of Andy Farrell, who always had a great work attitude, but others around him who were letting their standards slip.

I targeted players in Sydney who were available and brought in Robbie McCormack, the hooker Mark Bell, a wing man, and Danny Moore, a centre. They were all gold medallists in work ethics and this would rub off on the other players. As the season approached, we had again to look at small details such as how many were we to take on the team coach? Who was to go on the team coach? How big a coach did we need and what were the seats like? These were small things but were important if we were to reach away games in the best shape possible to win the game.

Then I targeted the newspapers. I had noted that public relations were not good; also that PR work was not Andy Goodway's strongest point, and I had to talk to him about that. He was a player who had played for me and often had gone beyond the call of duty. He was a player whose work ethic had been fantastic, but his bedside manner was poor! I felt we had seen enough bad publicity and it was time to get good stuff into the newspapers.

All this work had to be done before Monie could get down to working with the players. Some of the things he found were bordering on the crazy. For example, he found the club had two years' supply of kit stored at the JJB warehouse belonging to Dave Whelan! He had to show videos to the players in the cocktail lounge attached to the clubhouse. That aside, Monie and Marty Hulme got down to the hard graft which is pre-season training at any club.

The coach set to work on the technical side of things, leaving Hulme to handle fitness. One of the things he wanted to do was to get the stats men to convert players' work rates in attack and defence and to rate the players on a scale from one to ten for each phase. He only did it for a short time, but it did allow him, as he put it, to 'get down to the nitty-gritty' with players as individuals.

It is interesting to look at the training diary Monie kept for that period. While the players were working hard on fitness, Monie was also working hard on the technical side of the game. A typical session would contain a warm-up period, skills, defensive work right on left, left on right, penalty groups and tap groups. Equally, player input was involved. Robbie McCormack, the new Aussie hooker, wanted to introduce some numbers across the try-line, meaning the line was split into zones with each zone given a number. The thinking was if Robbie or Andy Farrell were to kick and called a number, all the team would know where the ball was going to be kicked. Then team-mates could tip each other off as to what they were going to do and where they would run to.

Once that practice was completed, Monie introduced a number of back-line moves involving what he referred to as 'unders' and 'overs'. Put simply, the player with the ball would either play under the defender, that is back on the defender's inside, or over, where he would try to get round the defender on the outside. Finally, they practised where they would take the rucks to allow moves to be carried out during a game, and where the best places were from which to attack a team.

If that was not enough, Monie finished the session with more technical information for the players, telling them of the need to have wider formation so that the backs and the back-row players could run in space when attacking. It was then on to the video ('I had introduced an "end on" camera which filmed play from behind the try line') for a session which showed players what they were doing wrong and, equally important, what they were doing right! Monie was jamming all this into the players in the first two months. It was testimony to his skill and the players' willingness to learn that it all began to gel so quickly. It was a demanding time for all concerned, and, in addition, Monie was still in the process of trying to sort out the huge squad he had inherited:

> As well as trying to get the technical side of things into the players, I was also trying to build a game plan with them, to try to instil in them how we were going to play our games. After I had been at the club a couple of months I was able, from what I had seen, to assess each of the players. I drew up three separate lists. The first was of the twenty players I felt could be starters for us as the season approached. The second was a list of seven players I thought could improve enough to play first grade, and finally I had ten or twelve I felt we could get rid of. The twenty starters I listed were: Radlinski, Bell, Robinson, Smythe, Cardiss, Connelly, Moore, Gilmour, Paul, Smith, Murdock, Cowie, Mestrov, Holgate, O'Conner, Betts, Haughton, Cassidy, Farrell and McCormack. Those who could develop were: Wes Davis, Dwaine West, Paul Johnson, Andy Johnson, Rob Ball, Mike Peters and John Clarke. I had a big question mark over Nigel Wright because of the bad injury he suffered.
>
> Those I was prepared to sell on were: Stuart, Roberts, Morris, Hanson, Barrow, Baynes, Whittle, Grundy, Whitehead, Lee, Hill, Hall and Talbot. I had to be so ruthless simply to get the squad down to a manageable size.
>
> That done, I then had to do some work on the opposition! I remember the first two clubs I looked at were Leeds and Castleford. Technically, I analysed where I thought they were strongest and weakest.
>
> The Challenge Cup competition had been switched

around as a result of Super League and was at the beginning of the season rather than at the end. That had its good side but it also had its downside. If you drew one of the weaker first division sides, it was good. On the other hand, if you drew a strong Super League club, it was bad. That year Leeds drew Castleford in the first round, and it turned out it was bad for Leeds; they lost.

For us it was good; we drew Keighley in the first round. It allowed us to put into a game what we had done on the training paddock. One of the journalists posed the question as we prepared for that first game: 'Will the magic return with Monie?' We were about to find out!

In that Keighley game I played Henry Paul at five-eight, started Stephen Holgate, and John Clarke played at hooker and went very well. I thought Jason Robinson went well, too, but I was looking to play him at half-back. I had it in my mind that during the season I would move him to half-back more frequently.

In the second round we drew Dewsbury, which was our second first-division opposition, so it was, again, a relatively easy match for us. Tony Smith came into the side, Jason Robinson was outstanding and Daryll Cardiss played very well. We were running good angles and off-loading well, which were the things we had been working on in training.

It was after those first two games that we had a bit of a setback. It was caused by the Wendall Sailor affair. John Martin, one of the directors, dropped the news of the so-called Sailor signing! Or non-signing, as it turned out to be! It was very embarrassing for me because I had spoken to Wayne Bennett, Sailor's coach, a week or so before the news conference and I knew nothing at all about the affair. It was a bombshell as I knew he was contracted to Brisbane. The whole episode was just a big mistake, which I guess ambitious people make! The club was desperate for good publicity after the two or three years of bad press and they desperately wanted to put something good in the papers. The three signings of McCormack, Moore and Bell were not regarded as big signings, and Wigan live on big signings. I think it was due to a couple of the directors saying, 'Well, we will throw in a big name!' because they did not have the faith that we could turn the club around in one season. So they were saying to people that whatever happens this season, we are going to sign big names for the next season! I was just embarrassed about the way the whole thing was done.

If that was not enough pressure, we had drawn St Helens in the cup! Fortunately we managed a good win. I remember Jason Robinson scored a try from inside our ten-metre zone, straight from a scrum, when he went the ninety metres. The game was tough; the first half, in particular, I would describe it as an 'Australian' first half. In the second half we played some good footy to win the game 22–10. The fans were happy as it was Saints and it was the cup, and I could see signs that the hard work we had put in was beginning to pay off. What I did not want, though, was for everybody to let 'the pats' on the back get to them. Whilst I was happy, there was still a lot to do. We had not been put heavily under pressure in a game. It is okay doing the right things in training, but we needed to do the right things in pressure situations in big games.

The response of all the players to the Monie regime was outstanding. Once again he had set about developing the 'team concept', just as he had in his first spell at the club. The players who had worked under him before relished the new approach, and Jason Robinson, Andy Farrell and Dennis Betts all hit top form at the beginning of the campaign. Off the field, the club signed a massive sponsorship deal with Tesco, and everyone began gearing up for a Challenge Cup semi-final against London

Broncos. It seemed that the good times were returning even sooner than Monie had anticipated. The club capitalised still further on the new-found goodwill by inducting recent favourite Shaun Edwards and wing legend Billy Boston into the newly instituted Wigan Hall of Fame.

London, inevitably, given the new spirit in the club, were easily dispatched and the club were back at Wembley stadium. The whole place was buzzing again. What pleased Monie about the semi win was the form of hooker Robbie McCormack. Monie felt his performance justified the faith he had had in him when he signed him. Equally pleasing was that Lee Gilmour and Paul Johnson were now beginning to perform in the way he had hoped. The bubble had to burst at some time, and Monie knew he had to be prepared when it did.

> I was pleased with the start, and we worked hard. I felt, though, that I wanted the team to play a bit more footy. They were making the hard yards up the middle and our completion rates for our sets of six were high. I felt that they were doing everything I was asking but seemed afraid to do any of the 'off the cuff' stuff which could break games. I had to loosen off a little and get them to take a few more chances on the paddock. Wembley was coming up and I knew it would be a big test for the boys, and so it proved to be.
>
> We did not play well. Early in the game Jason Robinson bombed a high kick and Sheffield scored. We compounded the error minutes later when Danny Moore played the ball, and Jason, who had just taken a knock, must have been looking the other way. The result was Sheffield regained the ball and took another set of six in front of our posts. They squeezed Matt Crowther in at the corner when Mark Bell came in off his wing. We lost 17–8, because Sheffield were good enough to hang on and take the game.

> My guys were not overawed by the occasion but we did make plenty of mistakes. I did feel it was not to be our day. Unlike losing a grand final in Australia, at Wembley I did not feel like I did not want to be there. We had achieved a great deal simply by getting to Wembley; Sheffield were too good for us on the day. I felt we really did not know how to win a tight game as yet; it was too early in the season. You know, the club had lost the winning habit over the last few years. Funnily enough we played Sheffield again the following week and flogged them!

Following Wembley, Monie sold wing man Rob Smythe to London and followed that up by losing yet another tight game. Wigan went to Headingley to play Leeds in what turned out to be a very good game, Monie's men going down 18–6. While not enjoying the loss, Monie was pleased with the performance. The intensity he was looking for was coming, but the salary cap was beginning to make its presence felt. The club had been made an offer for Daryll Cardiss, which in the end Monie put a block on. At that stage in the season he felt the player's speed might well be needed and with Smythe going it would leave the club short.

Monie found himself having more and more friendly arguments with Lee Gilmour, the youngster for whom he had high hopes. Gilmour felt he was a better centre than a back-row forward. Monie's view was that he was a back-row forward. Whoever was right was immaterial; Gilmour was beginning to make people sit up and take notice, much to Monie's delight.

He now began to shift the emphasis in training. Pleased with the form of McCormack, Monie began to work on the 'go forward' with the forwards; he placed even greater emphasis on teamwork and tried to increase the intensity of the play by stressing the need to play quality football. Just when smoother waters seemed to lie ahead, the storm broke once again:

> The chairman of the club, Mike Nolan, quit over the

Goldsphink deal. Sadly, I had a bit to do with that, along with John Martin. We did not tell anyone we were doing the deal, not even the chairman. That was something I had picked up from Maurice Lindsay. Wigan had attempted too many deals in the past that had not come off, and they had announced these in the paper before the deals had been done. You should always do it the other way, do the deal before it gets into the papers. It was not the best preparation for our 'on the road game'.

We played St Helens in Swansea. It was a game, looking back, which I thought was the turning point in our season. We played some great rugby league; it was a great game and one that I enjoyed. We targeted the Saints' full-back, Paul Atcheson. When we got into the last third of the field we were going to play two out from dummy half and run at their back line. Andy Farrell was to kick the ball along the ground behind them because we thought the full-back would be out of position. He was, and we won the game 36–2!

I can tell you, we all celebrated well that night, and I was 'helped' out of the bar in the early hours of the morning by Terry O'Connor and Tony Mestrov. They had been keeping their eye on me!

Some funny things happened between me and Terry O'Connor. I had him on edge: he did not know if he was good enough to play in the team, he did not know if he could make the sacrifices I required. I was always dropping him back to the bench; he always wanted to be starting. He was a player I loved to coach, he had plenty of character, he was always going to be in my team, but I did keep him on edge for a long time!

As I said, we really did kick on after the Saints game, but came a little unstuck towards the end of the season when we played Leeds at Central Park. Before that we played Sheffield again, this time at home, when we flogged them 44–6. I remember when the final whistle went, the thought that went through my head was, 'The bastards have still got the cup!'

Then it was Leeds. They beat us 15–8 in a tight one. Robbie McCormack was knocked out by Adrian Morley straight from the kick-off at the start of the game! I think everyone on the ground thought it was an illegal tackle, but referee Cummings didn't and to rub salt in the wound actually gave a scrum head and feed to Leeds. Then Mick Cassidy took retribution; he was sent off and got six matches which meant he would be out until the grand final, should we get that far.

I was pleased with the attitude of the players in spite of the loss. Andy Farrell, who was the skipper, was getting on to players to do the things we had practised in training. Even if we had scored a try, if Farrell thought we should have done something we had practised, one or two rucks before, he would get the players together and tell them the situation. I felt that Lee Gilmour, Paul Johnson and Stephen Holgate were emerging as our three aces in the pack. They were a little underrated by the opposition but I could see they were doing great things for us. More importantly I could see, as could the crowds, that the team was now winning 'the Wigan way'. Tony Smith and Henry Paul were becoming a very good combination at half-back. I felt it was time to kick up another gear if we were to get to the play-offs. We got the halfs to start to attack the opposition line a little more and we introduced little plays from first and second receivers, which we did when running at the defensive line.

Warrington was the last game of the regular season and sadly we lost Stephen Holgate, who dislocated a shoulder and would be out for the play-offs. This was a blow to us and it was a bit of a spiteful game. Jason Robinson got split open, and although we won 30–24, it was very tough. The win did secure top spot for us, so we could prepare for the play-offs knowing we would be at home whatever happened.

As it turned out, we played Leeds, and early in the week I decided to change our game plan again. We were going to play some football against them; we would shift the ball about the park. As it turned out, it rained on the night, which did not make for the best of conditions for the change of plan. I had a bit of a shudder to myself, but because the players were so confident that I had the answers, and we had practised all week shifting the ball in our own half, I stuck with it. I did not let the players see it, but I did roll my eyes when I looked outside at the wind and rain.

We were going to play football and it paid off; Gilmour scored the first try going ninety metres after we put four passes together on our own line. Bell got over from a Farrell kick. Terry O'Connor was starting to hit top form and it showed that night.

I decided that Cassidy was going to come back for the grand final. Holgate was out anyway, so it was Hobson's choice. I actually announced the team for the final a week and a half before the game, which was before the other finalist had been decided. I knew who our best seventeen players were and naming the team when I did had plenty of rub-offs for us. It showed the players I had confidence in them, the seventeen who were going to go to war. The unlucky guy was John Clarke, the hooker, who was eighteenth man, which is always tough. Some of the journalists took my action as being arrogant, but it was just that I had a belief in my players. It did also make the training sessions go a lot better.

I set about preparing a game plan for the final. At the start of the year I had a couple of signs put up in the dressing-room. One read: 'We must have the courage to confound expectations.' The second read: 'If you worry, you must convert that energy from worry to action. Worry will not prevent destiny from unfolding, however, self-effort has the power to change destiny.'

I told the players that during this grand final we needed to have clear vision, and we must hold the ball in two hands on contact. We would play the ball fast, have a good kicking game and chase every kick as a team. We would run more from dummy half and play for great field position. Also we would be tighter in defence and change the angles we would run. We could not simply play out our six tackles, so we needed to play for more off-loads. Finally, we were not going to be intimidated. Those were the things we drummed into the squad during that week and a half before the game.

On game day, when we were in the changing-room before the kick-off, I talked to the players about teamwork. I told them individuals play games and teams win championships and asked them how they could best help the team. We needed to play this game six tackles at a time; the team which made the fewest mistakes would get the opportunity to win the game. Every player had to take his chances, play to win and never, never give in, and make no excuses. I also told them to play the game not the event, and finished by telling them that 'All it takes is all you have got'.

When the game started we got plenty of blood bins which was good, because it allowed me to use more substitutions than the six allowed. Every time we played Leeds they were a tough physical contest and this time our front-rowers were bleeding straightaway, then Lee Gilmour got cut as well. That was good for me, as I said; it was not so good for the guys getting cut, but this was the grand final, so they did not mind!

The first big incident was when Marcella off-loaded to Newton, who in turn off-loaded to Harris, who made a bust down the middle. A quick play of the ball freed Blackmore because Danny Moore was just a little bit tight and could not get to him, and he scored. Just before half-time we put on a set play where Radlinski came off the second receiver. I remember at the time being disappointed because 'Rads' had no drop-off runner, no one came back on the angle against the grain. Radlinski ended up near the side line with Jason Robinson at dummy half. The rest is history: Jason scored from dummy half.

When I got the guys in the changing-room at half-time, I told them not to get caught up in the emotion of the event, particularly Mark Bell, who had played and lost a grand final in Australia, and young Lee Gilmour. We needed to have quicker formation on defence and make our tackles. I wanted them to have more 'speed sets' (where concentration is on quick play, the balls and people like Robinson running from dummy half).

In the second half Cowie carried on where he had left off in the first, and was our best prop that game. Although Andy Goodway didn't have a rap on him, I always thought he was our best prop. A little indiscipline began to creep into the Leeds game and I thought it cost them the game. There was nothing in the game; Leeds pounded us but we hung in there and toughed it out, and got the win. Andy Farrell said after the game, 'We learned how to win a tough one. John Monie has been a revelation to the players and has got us working together as a team.' My own thoughts went back to what the journalist had written at the start of the season and I have to say, 'The magic has returned'!

The magic had returned; the inaugural grand final had been won. Monie was the first man to win grand finals in both Great Britain and Australia, so how did he feel about completing this historic feat?

Looking back on it now that it is all over for me, that was probably one of my greatest achievements. But it is hard to

> separate stuff out. Every Wembley win was a great win, winning the championship, the Regal Trophy at Leeds, winning the Lancashire Cup at St Helens; anytime you win a big one it is great! But I had to start preparing for the next season.

During the off-season, the club sold Cardiss, Ellison, Nigel Wright, Hall and Tallec. Andy Johnson, who had picked up a bad injury, would miss the whole of the coming season, as would Dennis Betts. Lee Hanson and Craig Murdock were also allowed to leave, and it did not end there.

9

THE WIGAN ERA FINALLY ENDS

'If you worry, then divert that energy from worry to action. Worry will not prevent destiny from unfolding. However, self-effort has the power to change destiny.'

Monie may have won the grand final, but that was history by the end of the week. It had not stopped the club getting off-side with the authorities over breaches in the salary cap that had been introduced that season. To be fair, Wigan were not the only club to incur the wrath of the authorities, but they, like others, were struggling to get players' wages under the capping level. It was to have repercussions for Monie and lead to some harsh decisions. One such decision involved a crowd favourite at Central Park – stand-off Henry Paul.

> Wigan had been fined over the last few months of the season for salary-cap breaches. We certainly had some problems with it and we had to save some money in the new season. I had meetings with Dave Whelan and Peter Norbury, the new chairman, and it was decided that we had to get down under the salary cap. Letting Henry Paul go would save us a lot of money, but with hindsight I would

say it was not the smartest move we ever made. Henry had an option on his contract which meant that if we retained him he was eligible for a huge increase in salary, which we could not avoid. We were talking five figures and we simply could not sustain such an increase. This was a time when we had to cut back, not increase salaries, so, reluctantly, he was allowed to move to Bradford.

The salary cap had forced our hand a little. He wanted to play at Bradford with his brother, and it became increasingly difficult to hold him as the situation unfolded. Letting him go was something I regret; he has gone on to play some great rugby league for Bradford. Mind you, you often look back at things and say 'I would not have done that if I had known.' Trouble is you don't know!

I have always felt that imports should be backs and they should be game breakers, guys who could do things for the club. With Henry going, I saw Greg Florimo as that type of player.

Then we had a problem over Robbie McCormack. The chairman offered him an embarrassingly low amount of money for the new season, way below what he had been receiving when we won the final. I went to see Peter Norbury and got him to put another £10,000 on the offer but, by then, Robbie felt he had been insulted and did not re-sign.

We had to release a lot of players and I knew the squad was going to be thin. I told people we were really getting down to dangerous waters as we had only around twenty players, plus the good youngsters at the club. If we were to get a run on injuries we would be in trouble and this was exactly what happened at the start of that second season, with five first-grade starter players on the side line.

Guys like Stephen Holgate, who had been good for us, needed a shoulder operation and we let him go to Hull with Murdock, the half-back, in a transfer deal. We were dangerously short of players, that's for sure.

Problems were bubbling under the surface at the club, which I did not like. I had been arguing with the chairman, Peter Norbury, for quite a while. The squad was small. Central Park had been sold. We did not have anywhere to train but were at different venues at different times. Also they were getting ready to knock Central Park down. It was ridiculous; they were turning the lights out in the hallways. One day I came into training and the hot water had been turned off. This was to be a luxury for match days only! I called a plumber in, told him to turn it back on and said I would take the rap for it. It was not what I expected from a world-class club, but there were a lot of very petty things going on. They were letting Central Park run down but the players were still working there! On one occasion the players were taking a shower after training and the drains must have been blocked. As they showered the water backed up and the floor of the showers was covered in a green slime! Considering the fact that players to some extent are dependent on their feet, it was worrying to see this. I had to fight to get a plumber in to unblock the drains.

I have always felt you should conduct yourself with a bit of class and a bit of style, and we weren't doing that. Players did not know where they would be training from one day to the next. Dave Whelan was running the club from his office in JJB. I felt it was my job to defend the players because they should come first in any club. Training facilities and hot water should not be in question. We had been unsettled for some time. In that 1998 season we had had all the success on the field but were still having trouble with the chief executive. We started with Philip Clarke and as he went, Mike Nolan arrived. Then he went and, finally, Dave Whelan put Peter Norbury in charge.

He was a solicitor in Manchester and was only doing the job part time! He was only coming in every now and then;

> I think then they made Mary Charnock chief executive, so we had no continuity. The problems got worse as the season went on. They were trying to gear down from Central Park and get ready to go down to the JJB stadium. At the start of the season there was no groundsman at Central Park for six or eight weeks or so. The pitch was disgraceful; it was boggy and soft and had had no work done on it. The ground actually began to stink and players developed a rash after playing on it. We could not train on it. Our chief executive was part time, which made communicating difficult. We were not looking after things behind the scenes very well at all. We had just won the grand final.

It was not the way Monie did business, and it was not, in his view, the Wigan way. He tried all he could to shield the players from the back-room problems, but early in the season they were to see some of the problems first hand, and one of the players recalled this. It followed a match against Castleford at Central Park which Wigan lost. The chairman, Peter Norbury, actually got to the changing-rooms before the coach did, and as the player said: 'The chairman stormed into the dressing-rooms and hauled Andy [Farrell] and Jason [Robinson] out of the showers, demanding to know what had gone wrong, and why we had lost the game. When the coach arrived and saw this, he went ballistic and there was a stand-up row between the two. Things could have got out of hand, so Neil [Cowie] grabbed the chairman by the elbow and walked him to the door, telling him he was out of order.'

It was not the brightest thing the chairman could have done. Players are not happy when they lose and they expect their coach to perhaps shout at them (which Monie rarely, if ever, did). It was another matter for a non-rugby person to come into the dressing-room and shout at them. Peter Norbury was very lucky that he was escorted to the door; he could easily have found himself being thrown through it! The players were seeing for the first time some of the problems Monie faced behind the scenes. Monie, for his part, told the players that they were not to get off-side with the chairman or Dave Whelan. That was his job; theirs was to play rugby.

The constant battles that Monie had been involved in eventually took their toll:

> We were about two-thirds of the way through the season when Norbury called me into the office and sacked me! I remember I was very disappointed Dave Whelan had not supported me, but had chosen to support Norbury. I said at the time, 'All I have ever done for Wigan is win trophies and cups.' I was bitterly disappointed.
>
> I always knew that when we tried to get under the salary cap that injuries would hit us hard and we would have to tough it out through those times. They appointed Andy Goodway as coach and, as I said earlier, he was very set in his ways, and very abrupt with people. Andy got through to the end of the season and then he was gone.
>
> I felt it was a sad way to end what, for me, had been one of the happiest and most productive coaching periods of my career. I still felt that the decision to return to Wigan was the best I ever made in my career. We had a fantastic first season and it ended with me getting sacked. Maybe my only crime was bringing success back to the club too soon, giving them success again before they were ready for it. One thing was for certain; I had fought the chairman and lost.

It is somewhat ironic that a few months later Norbury himself was to leave the club, replaced by Maurice Lindsay. The club had turned full circle. Sadly, time had moved on and there was not to be a third comeback for the master coach.

10

THE LONDON BRONCOS

'You do not have to have been a horse to be a jockey!'

Again, Monie found himself out of work, and again, he felt pretty hard done by. The situation was, though, of his own making. He had forced Dave Whelan to make a decision, to choose between his coach or his chairman. He chose the chairman! After all, Wigan had won the inaugural grand final and were well on course to make the play-off stage again. Such success was, for some reason, not enough for the chairman, Peter Norbury. Wigan did make it to those play-offs, staging their sudden-death eliminator not at Central Park but at the new JJB stadium. The visitors were Castleford and they outplayed Wigan to take the semi. It was not an auspicious start at the new stadium, and ultimately cost Andy Goodway his job.

However, things were happening. Norbury was soon to leave to be replaced by Maurice Lindsay, who was to return as chairman and chief executive. His coming was too late to save Monie. Other offers did come to Monie because, after all, he was the most successful coach in the history of the English game.

Hull wanted Monie to take over the coaching role at the

Boulevard, but the situation there was, to put it mildly, somewhat volatile. The club did not know if they would be playing in the Super League in 1999 or dropping down to the Northern Ford Premiership (NFP). The financial situation was precarious, but Monie recognised there was young talent which was coming through at the club. The problem was that the talent was not yet ready for the rigours of Super League. Had the club been relegated to the NFP Monie would have been tempted to take the job and, hopefully, nurture the youngsters through to promotion; that extra year would have helped the younger players enormously.

> The thing about Hull was they knew they were going back to the first division. They [the NFP] offered me the job, so I would handle recruitment and the development of the good young players they had there. They felt they would be back in Super League in twelve months. It was a job needing an eye for development. I went over there and met with a couple of people connected with the club, looked at a few places we could live and so on. At the end of the day they could not offer me anything concrete; they didn't really know what was going to happen with the Gateshead thing! As it turned out, had I accepted the job rather than the London offer, I would have been out anyway. Once Gateshead took over, or 'merged' as the rugby league authorities put it, they had a coach in place with Shaun McCrea. So although Hull could not guarantee me anything, I felt it was such a great rugby league area, and the job was very attractive to me.

Sadly, the situation was so unsettled on Humberside that when a second club, London Broncos, came to talk with him, he decided to move to the capital. London were on their third coach in a year and Monie felt that stability was needed. He knew that they would be playing Super League in 1999. Whilst they had stability, relatively speaking, off the field, he hoped he had what was needed on the paddock.

In some respects it proved to be the right decision, because soon the bombshell dropped. Gateshead, who had been admitted to Super League the previous season in a fanfare of publicity and talk of expansion of the game, suddenly were no more. They had lost over £700,000 on the season and announced that they were to merge with the Hull club. McCrea, who was the Gateshead coach, would take over the new Hull set-up but the Australian players would be allowed to play for the new club. The rules were 'amended' to enable Hull to play with fifteen import players for their first season, a privilege until then only afforded London and the now defunct Paris club. Monie felt his decision to move to London had been justified, arguing a bird in the hand was worth two in the bush. Had he waited for the Hull job he may well have missed out on the London one, and there was no guarantee he would have been offered work at Hull, given the changing circumstances at the club.

So it was that Monie moved to the capital in preparation for the 2000 Super League season.

> When I took over at London I made what was probably one of the most stupid comments of my coaching career when I said I felt London were a top-five outfit! I had seen them from far away in the north the season before and they always struck me as a top-five club. I said that, not realising that the playmakers in Peter Gill, Shaun Edwards and Martin Offiah were either leaving the club or had already done so. My philosophy has always been if you have a guy who is always up among the leading try-scorers, then you don't let him go.
>
> With hindsight, one of the problems at the Broncos

was a lack of penetration in the team. If someone could bust a hole, or even wedge a bit of a hole, in the opposition there was nobody left there who could get over the line regularly. Martin, as everyone knows, could always get over the line, could always find a try. He went to Salford and we played them four times; in three of the games we were beaten by Martin Offiah tries. In the last game against them he let the players know to tell the management there were still plenty of tries left in him!

It was only when Monie arrived in the capital that he saw first hand the enormity of the task that confronted him. If coming into Wigan had been difficult, London was almost insurmountable.

The problems were pretty complex. When I got down to London I moved into Tony Rae's place temporarily over at Twickenham. That was where all the players, staff and management were based. We got through a month of pre-season work; then we had a window of about two weeks when everyone had to move from west London to the other side of the city. It was disruptive; many of the players and their families did not settle, Karl Hammond the captain for one. Later it came out in stages that they hated living in south London and could not wait to get back up north and away from the capital. Moving forty players, wives and kids, plus the support staff, and finding them all houses, was very, very disruptive.

We took over a rugby union club, knocked down one of the walls of a squash court and tried to set up a gym. All the equipment had to be transported across London to the new gym. The coaching staff were housed in a ten-foot-square room with no window, along with the video equipment. The physio worked out of one of the little changing-rooms. The fields were disgraceful. It was one hell of a move. Kelvin Giles was not happy about the move at that point in time because it was when he wanted to work the players hard in preparation for the new season. In spite of all that, my personal belief was that the south-east of London and Charlton was the right place for the club to be.

Once I knew about the move I should have said to everyone that it was going to be a transitional year. But before I got there I had made the stupid statement that we were going to be a top-five outfit. It certainly came back to haunt me because there was no way we were ever going to make the top five.

There were a lot of problems off the field; there were more, though, when I began to look at the team. Gill had gone and Karl Hammond was not happy, but we did pick up a half-back, and, as I have always said, it is half-backs who make great teams. We got Brendan Magnus from Balmain (who was to damage his cruciate ligament very early in the season). Shaun Edwards was running on old legs and was a tired player. He had been through a lot and I certainly agreed with his decision to retire. It left us in a very vulnerable position, however, and we had to bring in another half-back, so brought Glenn Air over again, having released him at the end of the previous season!

We had no penetration in our back row, which is something I believe is essential in a team, but instead had smaller, front-row-type players in the back row! I began to look around to see if there was a footballer on the market who could run the football. We picked up Paul Davidson, who fitted the bill physically and was a player who could make an impact. He was explosive, physically and mentally, which I knew we had to have somewhere in the side.

I went back to Wigan and did a deal with Maurice Lindsay, who had returned as chairman and chief executive, and brought John Clarke and Andy Johnson to the club. Wigan thought both players were below the level of playing excellence required at Wigan, but they were still easily fitted into the London set-up. They and Shaun Edwards were among the best trainers, early in the season, which comes back to that Wigan education we talked about. They trained the place down, so much so that young Clarke developed a stress fracture of the leg and we had to start the season without him. Andy Johnson looked as if he could made the loose-forward role his own. I realised quickly that the side was always going to be a battling side; we were always going to have to try to grind out wins.

In trying to increase the size of our pack, we picked up Justin Dooley, who turned out to be our best buy. He won all the prizes at the end of the season and was a guy who would not be out of place in one of the sides up north.

It is worth noting here that when the London Broncos held their awards evening, four or five weeks after Monie's departure, Dooley actually thanked Monie in his absence for making him the player he had become at the club. He felt Monie had improved his game so much and was grateful for the opportunity to work under him. It was a speech which did not go down well with the directors and chief executive. Mind you, one gets an impression of just what Monie was up against when you see who won the club Man of the Year award: it went to the club accountant! That, though, should not have surprised anyone, for the previous year the same award had been won by a club director.

Dooley was very good for the club. Scott Cram was still developing his game. Steele Retchless and Shane Millard were to become the regular back-row forwards, and you would not find more honest and hard-working forwards anywhere. But the balance of the pack was not tipped towards being successful.

I am afraid these were the problems I inherited when I arrived, and they were problems in areas where I have always liked my teams to be strong. The qualities required were not present at the Broncos, so I knew we were always going to struggle and we were always going to be hanging on, trying to win games.

The pre-season training proved tough for Monie, with problems both off the training pitch and on it. The training pitches were of a poor standard and Monie was to have more than one argument with the groundsman at the rugby club where they were stationed. There was a boggy patch along the bottom end of one field – grass was not cut, and Monie described it as a field which looked like a horse show had been on it. The training staff kept trying to address the problems, but were getting little co-operation from the groundsman. Monie recalled his last argument with the guy:

> After the last row he said to me, 'What you need is a soccer pitch to train on.' I said, 'If you mean I am looking for something flat with a covering of grass on it, then, yes, that is what I want.' Finally, halfway through the season, they put drainage right through the playing field paid for with Broncos' money. We were supposed to be back on the field in six weeks, instead we could not get on it and the season ran out on us! That was twelve weeks of training on the number-two field and there were channels every ten metres down the field which were filled with sand. It seemed like every week a player would step in the bloody sand and hurt an ankle! It was very disruptive.

Disruptive was putting it mildly. It was a situation Monie did not expect, and it was a situation one would not expect to find at a Super League club. Monie admitted to being shocked at the state in which he found the club, and, unfortunately, the problems ran right through; they were not just at first-grade level. This was despite the club receiving a vast amount of money from News Corporation via the Super League Europe organisation!

> The back-up talent in the club was not in reserve grade; it was in the under-18 side. With the injuries we were picking up we could not put any pressure on the first-grade players. It was the first time in my coaching career that I was not in a position to drop players. There was no one else with the talent to come up.

The whole club was not in the best of shape, and the season was fast approaching. The team were on the wrong side of a lot of close decisions in the early games. They came close to winning but lacked that touch of class to take the game the full distance and win. Wigan came down to the capital and London ran them very close before losing in the last ten minutes or so by 16–12. St Helens came and again London were leading the Saints until five minutes from the end. Saints got up to steal the game by 26–20. Monie felt that the opposition were not winning games, London were losing them. It boiled down to an education thing, players were playing dumb football when the pressure was on in matches. In those situations coaches need to work with players over a period of time to get them out of those habits. Monie was aware of the cold reality:

> All the close decisions come up as losses on the win–loss sheet. At the end of the day, when the directors decided they had to do something, their decision was to sack the coach. When it ended and I was sacked, I was very disappointed because I felt the club had not been very

> fair. They had been through five coaches in a couple of seasons and that was just a stupid way to run a rugby league club. When I signed my contract with Tony Rae I signed for two years, but the contract had been written up by the people at Virgin. It had a clause in there which when I took legal advice I was told was an old legal trick, a technicality. The start of the contract said it was for two seasons but when you read the fine print there was a get-out clause saying they only had to give you three months' notice. In essence, when I was talking to Tony Rae and saying the club needed some stability (which he agreed with), all along he knew, in truth, I had only signed a three-month contract!

The facts did not stack up on two fronts: match statistics and player recruitment for the 2001 season. The board had supported Monie in his efforts to build a squad for the forthcoming season which he felt he could mould into a challenger for a top-five place. It was a process of rebuilding which he had instigated half-way through the season. He knew where the problems were in his squad and began to try to bring in players who would strengthen the club for the 2001 season. This he did with the backing of a board which weeks later was to sack him, thus denying him the opportunity to stand or fall with a squad he had put together. As Monie said, he had to narrow the talent gap.

> Like all coaches, we got information sent through from players' agents. Tony Rae and I both received these kinds of details and so began compiling a list of players who were coming up and available. I sat down with Tony and told him, we are lacking penetration, we are lacking back-line players who can make breaks. We are lacking creative forwards who can use the ball. Then I worked up a team I thought would win football matches. As I recall I had a

shortlist of ten or twelve players, in positions we needed to strengthen, which I passed to Tony Rae.

He played around with them on a blackboard, sort of like a fantasy league, to see how they all fitted in. Where, for example, could we have a little bit of explosion in the back row, penetration from our back line? Tony's next plan was to start phoning these players, but I advised him that was not the way to do it. He had to get on a plane, fly to Australia and do it in person. I had seen Ian Robson at Auckland and Maurice Lindsay at Wigan do business that way, to great effect. We had a meeting with Ian Burrows of Virgin, and David Hughes, and I suggested this to them and they agreed. Tony should get on a plane and go ahead and do it. When he came back he had signed six or seven of the players I had recommended. It was a job well done.

Monie knew the 2000 season was going to be tough, but he was well under way with his plans for it. He was not to be allowed the opportunity to work with the squad he had assembled.

That was the stupidity of the whole thing. Having listened to me, and allowed Tony to go to Australia to sign these players, they sacked me. It did not make sense to me; it did not make sense to a lot of rugby league people. But then when you have a look at people who have a bit to do with sport in England – directors and chairmen, who are put in position for non-rugby league reasons, then their decisions will not make sense.

When you look back, Les Kiss and Tony Rae had done some coaching the year before me, also Tony Currie and Dan Staines, but by the time the season was coming to an end those people weren't there any more; they had gone. So there was no one looking after the next season. That is why, when I signed the two-year contract, I told them one of the things the club needed was stability in the coaching ranks. It is that which makes the situation very absurd.

I feel I should not point the finger at individuals, but I would say that any team would find a spot for players like Steele Retchless. He was the Mike Cassidy of the London Broncos. As it turned out, he was the guy we were banking on to win us a game, when really he should not have had that role.

We did try to strengthen the squad during the season but we could not get players to come down from the north! We kept in touch with players who were disgruntled at their clubs, and those clubs were prepared to release. We got into a few loan deals but players who come like that certainly bring excess baggage with them. Moving to London was a huge decision for players in the north. To be quite honest about it, they didn't want to do it; the living expenses were too high for them. A £20,000 contract seemed high, but in the capital you just could not survive on it!

When the end-of-season statistics were examined for the Super League clubs there are some interesting comparisons. London were in the top three clubs for tackles made during the season. They were also involved in the game which had the most tackles made in it throughout the season. Kicks in general play saw the club again in the top three; for kicks regained, grubber kicks behind the defensive line, attacking kicks in play, they were rated as one of the top two teams, while for off-loads marker-defence tackles, they were in the top two or three. There were a great many aspects of the game where the coaching skills of Monie came through. However, in the ratings for the top fifty players for the season there were only two Broncos players listed: Karl Hammond and Justin Dooley. It seems individuals were not rated highly but the team was actually performing up there with the best of them; a coach could ask no more.

As Monie said, he had a proven track record and yet the club still slipped in the get-out clause that turned his supposedly two-year contract into, effectively, a three-month one. That was not the action of a club which is looking for stability, rather one which was hedging its bets.

> I tried to give the club a little bit of stability; they needed someone who knew how to recruit and so on. I thought I could make London successful, that is why I was so disappointed at the way it ended. With the new players coming in they had every right to be successful, simply because of the team we put together for 2001. What had happened in the past was that the coaches were planning to put next season's team together as their present season was ending. When you look back, Les Kiss and Tony Rae had done some coaching the year before me. Also Tony Currie and Dan Staines, but by the time the season was coming to an end those people weren't there any more; they had been sacked. So there was no one looking after the next season. That has never been my way. I have always thought that if you don't recruit until the end of the season then you are six months too late. You have to do your recruitment in the middle because by the time the halfway mark comes up, you should have a fair idea of strengths and weaknesses. Then you get in and get it done, or other teams start and you lose out. That is what has happened for so long at London. By the time they were ready to recruit, they had sacked their coach. When the new guy arrived there were few, if any, players available!

Rugby league has a long history of turning its back on its heroes, be they players or coaches. It will be a long time before we see again the likes of Ellery Hanley, Dean Bell, Martin Offiah, 'The Crow', Ray Price, Brett Kenny, Peter Stirling and so on. It will also be a long time before we see a coach of John Monie's calibre again, if ever. It is sad that he was unable to leave the game he has graced for over forty years under his own terms, in his own way. That, while not overly worrying him will sadden him.

11

LINDSAY'S VIEW

It was early in 1980, when Maurice Lindsay joined the board of the Wigan club, that they were at their lowest ebb. The club was about to be relegated to the second division, crowds were extremely poor, and there was a good chance that financial problems would see the end of the world-renowned outfit. The famous Wigan walk had been performed many times during that troubled season which had seen the club relegated. Now there were so few supporters attending the matches it was in danger of becoming the Wigan 'trickle' rather than the 'flood' it had once been. The situation was dire, and about to get worse, as Lindsay recalled:

> When I joined the board, the bank manager was actually considering whether he should process three cheques issued by the club. Harry Gostelow, who was the chairman at that time, came round to my office and said the board would like to extend an invitation to me to join them. Incidentally they invited Jack Robinson to join them on that same day. The reason was that Ian Clift and Tom Bennett had both resigned as they were fed up with things.

> I joined the board thinking it was an honour, not realising the bank was not processing the cheques! I thought it was a little strange when at the first meeting they made me finance director, but only when I visited the bank did I realise the true horror of the picture.

Lindsay quickly learned that the board of twelve directors was too large and unwieldy; changes needed to be made if the club was simply to survive:

> The board meetings were not getting anywhere. They would start at 6.00 p.m. on a Monday night and go on until midnight, and a great deal of it was simply hot air. The agenda even included 'critical letters from spectators', so it was obvious the administration of the club had no authority; everything had to go through the board. Also the board were reluctant to give up any power. We could spend an hour and a half arguing about what size wheelbarrow to buy!
>
> Jack Robinson and I had a talk about the situation and then extended the conversation to Tom Rathbone. Jack Hilton also said he would like to be part of any reduced board. We had to put a motion forward to reduce the size of the board, but Jack felt it would go through. It was resisted by others, people like Martin Ryan and Alf Close, but the motion was finally carried.

So was born the so-called 'Gang of Four': Jack Robinson, Jack Hilton, Tom Rathbone and the chairman Maurice Lindsay. They would form a new streamlined board of directors, a format which has since been copied successfully by a number of other so-called 'Super League' clubs.

Success, albeit somewhat modest, quickly followed. The club gained promotion from the second division after only one season languishing in the lower echelons of the game. As Lindsay said:

> We first had to go into that second division because we had not yet been relegated when I joined the board. It was hard to get out of that division. Fulham started that same year, York had a dammed good side and the likes of Swinton and Blackpool were as good as we were at that time. We didn't have a cast-iron guarantee we would come back up. In fact, we came back up in second place eventually.

In fact, it was York that were promoted as champions at the end of that 1980–81 season. They were followed up by Wigan, the newly formed Fulham and Whitehaven. A series of coaches came and went at Wigan as Lindsay searched for the right formula that would bring the success he desperately wanted.

> George Fairbairn coached the club in the second division and was then replaced by Maurice Bamford, who in turn was followed by Alex Murphy. All contributed to the club in completely different ways. But we had not reached the level I felt we needed to be at to achieve greatness again. The next progressive step was to bring in Colin Clarke in tandem with Alan McInnes. Alan brought a studious approach to the job while Colin brought a bright mind and a great deal of passion. He was very committed and between them they gave us sincerity and intellect, and it worked well. However, we were still a long way behind the southern-hemisphere clubs. Every time I went to the southern hemisphere I saw that they were playing a different game, and I mean a different game. They had full-backs and half-backs who were kicking! Ours never kicked; they would simply collect the ball and take the tackle.

Whilst it was inevitable that Lindsay would go for a coach from down under, the appointment of New Zealander Graeme Lowe was to prove to be a masterstroke. It was a move that was to trigger the sustained success Lindsay sought. Even today, he still considers the Kiwi Lowe to be almost an evangelist in the way in which he introduced new ideas into the game in England. Lowe brought to Central Park what Lindsay wanted, that is many of the ideas he had witnessed in Australia, to create a team which won matches, played attractive rugby and brought in the crowds. Crowds meant money, money meant financial problems faded away, money meant the ability to bring in more players, world-class players. It was Lowe who ushered in the era of the full-time professional rugby league player, and that cost money. Lindsay was prepared to take that risk, because what was important was success on the field. If that came then the rest would fall into place. The culmination of Lowe's success came on 7 October 1987. The event was the World Club Challenge.

The champions of Australia were playing the champions of Great Britain for the right to call themselves champions of the world. This inaugural World Club Challenge was to be played at Central Park, Wigan, and the opponents were Manley–Warringah from Sydney. This was at a time when the game in England and the game in Australia were light years apart. No one really believed that such a match would even be competitive, nobody, that is, except Lindsay. It was the first of many magical nights he was to be involved in during his time at Wigan. He, along with 36,895 spectators, crammed into the ground by the River Douglas to see Wigan triumph 8–2 against all the odds. People witnessed that night a passion within the English game that had been missing for almost two decades. It was the kind of atmosphere Lindsay was to come to relish. It was also the beginning of the most successful period in the club's history.

The club had always had great players and even great teams. They were, after all, the most successful club in the history of the game. What they had never done was to dominate the game in this country in such a way, and for so long. Maurice Lindsay was to build a dynasty at Central Park which would see fifteen years of unparalleled success. It is a tribute to his ability that success was not only achieved during his reign, it continued long after he left the club to become chief executive of the Rugby Football League.

This success, like many things in life, could so easily have turned out to be very different. Events occur, opportunities present themselves; sometimes you grasp them and success follows. Sometimes you miss the opportunity, or make the wrong decision, and suddenly success is sailing down the river and you are helpless to do anything about it. Lindsay found himself in just that very position. Graeme Lowe, the successful Kiwi coach, decided to return to the southern hemisphere. Lindsay revealed:

> It all came out in the wash later, but Lowe was actually poached by Ken Arthurson, who was over here for an international board meeting being held at the same time as the Wembley Cup final. Ken asked Graeme if he would like to come to Manly. Graeme at the time was still under an 'unwritten' contract with us at Wigan. He left us a year early and we wondered why. He said he wanted to see his kids in Australia. But soon after arriving in Sydney we found he had been installed as the Manly coach. The truth of the matter only came out later.

So the search was on to find a replacement. Lindsay realised it was not simply a replacement for Lowe who was needed, even that would be nigh on impossible. No, what was needed was a coach who would take the players, the team, the club, to an even higher plane, even greater success. This success would rival that of the Aussie clubs who were playing in the greatest comp in the world. One accusation which could never be levelled at Lindsay was that he was a shrinking violet when it came to goal setting. (It was after all that approach, which had been so successful at Wigan, that was to lead Lindsay into deep water once he attempted to adopt it as chief executive of the Rugby League.)

He was not alone in seeing what had been achieved in his time at the club, but he alone realised it was not enough. He alone was not prepared to sit back on his laurels and bask in the reflected glory. If the club, his club, was to consistently match the Australian clubs then it needed to move on, not just to the next level but probably two or three levels higher. This, after achieving the ultimate accolade of being crowned World Club Champions! If this progress was to be made then it was important, even vital, that the right coach was brought in to replace the departing Graeme Lowe. Where was he to find such a man? Was there such a man? It was just the kind of problem Lindsay relished.

Whilst the club had experienced success, it was, in Lindsay's view, due to the influence of the southern hemisphere and the high-quality coaches which the Australian league produced. So it was then inevitable that he would return down under for his new coach, a coach who would need to share his vision for the club. A vision which was one of success both on and off the field. To achieve this needed careful planning and a great deal of investigation. As it turned out, it also needed a great deal of persuasion on Lindsay's part. Luckily this was an area he was good, even gifted, at.

> It was disappointing to lose Graeme at that time and I realised that we needed an Australian coach. I had always been a big Parramatta fan and went to the club when I was down under. I had actually brought Brett Kenny to Wigan from there in 1984. When down under I usually stayed with one of the club officials, John White. I suppose John was a forerunner of your modern-day agent; he advised players like Brett and Peter Sterling about their affairs. After the game I would always go into the Parramatta dressing-room. John Monie was Jack Gibson's assistant when I first went there and then took over from him as

head coach.

I simply noticed this very quiet, modest man in the dressing-room who clearly had the respect of all the players. I thought it impressive that he could command respect with such a demeanour. The month Lowe left Wigan, strangely enough, John Monie was saying he was not going to do another year with Parramatta, having been there nine years as assistant and then head coach. I thought this was just too good a coincidence to be true.

I rang John White and told him we needed a coach, that two or three names had come up and we definitely wanted an Aussie as I felt there were no coaches of similar status in England. I also told him we had experienced two years of success but we needed to kick on. I ended by asking him what he thought of John Monie.

Instantly, he told me, 'He is brilliant.' I remember asking him, 'How do you compare him to Brian Smith?' We had considered Smithy when Lowe had taken the job, as we now know, at Manly. White's answer was, 'Different. He will get the respect of all your players and coaching staff by his quiet modesty; he certainly will not take you backwards!'

With that, I had made up my mind. I asked him to have a word with Monie for me. White duly did, and the answer came back that he was not interested in coming to England, so I asked if I could have a word with him myself because I was not going to give up the battle so easily. When I did manage to speak with him, John Monie was adamant, 'No, I have had nine years of training and coaching. I want to take a year out.'

I let it go at that, but rang him back a few days later introducing myself as 'the nuisance from England'. I stressed I really would like him to come and it would be a good salary. I told him I didn't know what he was on, but I would match it, and there would be a nice house on the outskirts of Wigan, plus a car.

It was then I sensed a weakening as John replied, 'Jeezz, man, I would have to think about it. We have never really left Australia before. I have had a week in Bali, surfing. Is Wigan anything like Bali?' (It was said as a joke.)

I hesitated before replying, 'Well, in a different way you could find the same pleasures.' I had not got a clue what I meant by that, but I had him rocking a little now, got him thinking about it.

I rang him back a couple of days later, asked if I was speaking to the 'next Wigan coach' and told him I thought he should come. It would be a fresh life, a new start which would blow away the staleness of Parramatta. I told him we had a great set of players here whom he would enjoy working with. I asked him to have a word with Brett Kenny and the players who had been here before. We had looked after the Aussie players so well I had no doubt they would sell the club just as well as I could. I batted his brow and eventually persuaded him to come.

It has to be said that the methods adopted by Lindsay did not meet with universal approval, not even among the Wigan public. There were those who felt that he had too much power at the Wigan club. Equally, it must be said, there were those who would give him the freedom of the borough simply because he was turning the club around and making it great once more. It is a philosophy which he has not changed. As chief executive at the Rugby League he was often accused of riding roughshod over opposition, not suffering fools lightly, wanting his own way, being selfish, rude, egotistical and many other things according to the average supporter's view. It never bothered him! Lindsay is a gambler, a man who is prepared to back his own judgement, and he did so in the case of Monie. It must be said it worked.

It turned out to be a marriage made in heaven, really. We

got on like a house on fire. I was best man at his wedding and godfather to his little girl after she was born.

The former Wigan chairman (first time around!) has no doubt just what it was that Monie brought not only to the Wigan club but also to the game in England.

Graeme Lowe had taken us down the track, no doubt about that, but he had not finished the job off. He had made the players think differently, and be aware of how the game played in Australia was different. He was a very passionate man and a lot of his success was almost spiritual. He was, before his ill health, a very convincing and charismatic speaker and he would make people really believe in him and in themselves. That caused us to dominate the game here. But he did not coach in an intricate, technical way, as John Monie was to do. John brought technical expertise. Whilst he did not make rousing speeches, he got conviction into the side because of his quiet determination. John blended well with the work Lowe had done in his three years; he was the perfect follow-up. If we had brought in another firebrand it may well have confused the players, but John came with a very circumspect reflective manner, and, I would have to say, because he was a rugby league expert it meant we got the best of both worlds. We got the revival through Graeme Lowe and the completion through John Monie.

John was brilliant at dealing with players who had big egos, yet did not upset them or other players. We had Edwards and Gregory the half-backs, as different as chalk and cheese. Hanley a quiet man's man; Offiah flamboyant, a real showman; Lydon in the centre; and Hampson who at times was too brave for his own good. We had enormous egos all round the place and rightly so because they were all champions in their own right. In the pack we had

Skerrett, Platt, Dermot, Betts and Clark. It was a myriad of stars at the club when John came in.

John blended them and he handled them expertly. He was able, in a calm dignified way, to tell a player why he was being dropped. He did it in such a gentle, expert and manly way that the player would accept his views. He would sometimes give a player a tape and say, 'I am not going to play you, and that's the reason.' His real skill was to tell players a couple of weeks earlier, 'I am not really happy with what you are doing. I want you to do this or I will have to change things.' Usually the players responded and he had his brilliant thirteen out on the park week after week.

Also, because he did not seek the limelight, because he did not put himself in front of the players, they would accept that what he said was always truthful. Very few players, if any, during his time at this club had a bad word to say about him.

Lindsay is quick to acknowledge the influence Monie exerted outside the dressing-room as well as in it. He and Monie had developed an almost telepathic 'brotherhood', as it were.

I knew him so well and liked him so much; we complemented each other. I did not have one hundredth of his rugby league technical knowledge, but he respected my ability to recognise players who would blend into the side and he allowed me to buy players; he trusted my judgement. I managed to bring in players, although I would talk to John first and get his support, but he allowed me to use my imagination to acquire them.

For example, I knew we were one player short to make us the greatest British rugby league side ever, and that player was Martin Offiah. We had everything except that unique Olympian speed on one of the wings. Putting

Offiah and Gene Miles together was one of the greatest partnerships ever! In that respect John trusted me.

On another occasion I remember, when John had only been here a few weeks, we were to lose Adrian Shelford and Kevin Iro for fifteen weeks. They had to join the New Zealand team that toured not only this country but also France. Under the stupid law at that time we had to release them for northern hemisphere tours, which was barmy because we were paying them. I told John we were to be two players down. He said he knew a couple of players, a couple of reserve grade players from Parramatta who would do a job.

I thought, 'I don't want a couple of reserve-grade players,' so I said, 'No, John, this is Wigan. We don't sign reserve-grade players from anywhere or play anybody just to do a job. We sign the very best of internationals in every spot if they are proven, or the best top juniors, whom we will then groom for the top.'

John simply said, 'I was just trying to save you a bit of money.' I told him not to worry about that; it was my job to find it. We brought in Phil Blake and Les Davidson and they had fifteen great weeks with us. That incident I think showed to John that my approach was the same as his; there was no need for compromise ever. I think at the end of the day it was a case of each knowing the other knew his own job, and both he and I were ambitious. From then on we were always on the same wavelength.

I remember one day in Australia having a Chinese meal with John and the then coach of North Sydney. The coach asked John what he thought of a particular player and John just laughed and said, 'Ask Maurice; he is a better judge than me!' That is just the sort of modest way he has about himself.

Yet another skill Monie had which impressed Lindsay was his

ability to build a side that would have permanence. He was always looking ahead, always looking to the future. Equally, though, Lindsay felt he was always willing to give youngsters an opportunity. He would put them in a protected environment, making sure the side was strong enough to look after them. It mattered not if they were Andy Gregory or Gene Miles or A.N. Other; they all got the same respect from John.

Monie had one other quality which made him uncannily like his chairman:

> He had a high work rate; he went on the bus with the team to every reserve-grade game; he was part of the set-up. You were lucky to get the likes of Alex Murphy at a first-grade training session, never mind an away team game in reserve grade! Murphy didn't have a clue who was in the A team. John would go on the bus to Hull and get home at 1.00 a.m. He respected players and he worked with players.

During their time together Lindsay cannot remember a time when they ever disagreed on any aspect of what was best for Wigan.

There was, though, a third element at the club, namely the captain, be it Ellery Hanley or the Kiwi, Dean Bell. Lindsay readily acknowledged their contribution:

> Dean Bell was a great captain, as was Ellery. There is no doubt about that. Dean brought steely discipline to the team. For example, one incident I remember when we signed Martin Offiah. He came into the dressing-room with a bag which was twice the size of anyone else's. He was told where to get stripped but when he put his bag down on his spot it extended over onto Dean's spot. Dean came in and even before welcoming him to the club simply said, 'Shift that bag. Everybody has their own space here and we don't take over someone else's space.' Only then did he shake his

hand and welcome him to Wigan.

I also remember when Neil Cowie came Dean would not let him train the first day because he was too scruffy. He had a scruffy shirt on so was told to get out. If you train here you train like a champion and you dress like a champion! Dean had a very good relationship with John, but do not forget it was not just Dean, Ellery was very close to John also.

Both Ellery and Dean were inspirational, both were incredibly dedicated trainers, tough athletes who never admitted to pain, and both carried out John's instructions on the field to the letter.

With those two players, chairman Lindsay was able to extend his own ideas not just into the dressing-room but also onto the pitch. Chairman, coach, captain and, ultimately, the team were pulling in the same direction. As the chairman noted:

> I read recently in one of the sports newspapers that there was no team spirit at Wigan in the days we were winning everything. The writer did not know what he was talking about; there was a unique team spirit at the club.
>
> It was based on a desire to win but it was a collective will. Of course, Gregory was unique; he always had been from age eleven. Edwards was another unique individual and has been since he was six! Offiah, Bell . . . the list was endless. What Monie gave them was immense confidence in each other. When you go into war, which sometimes is what rugby league is akin to, your own confidence and courage improve because you are surrounded by so many heroes. John loved that. He was part of that; he was one of them!

During the time the chairman and the coach were together, there were many great achievements. However, Maurice Lindsay is in no doubt just what Monie's greatest ever achievement at Central Park was:

It was John and Ellery Hanley combining. We had a fantastic year when we won everything we could. Being so professional, John wanted to win the league more than anything else. You know, he considered cups to be competitions which fly by, but the league is a test of your everyday ability. Because of the fixture congestion brought about by our success, we were faced with playing four games in six days.

We had to play at home to Castleford on the Sunday. We had to play at home to Widnes, who were third in the league, on the Tuesday. We were at home to Bradford on the Thursday and away to Leeds on the Saturday. We had to play on a Saturday because Granada television were covering the games then on *RL Live*.

John gambled slightly against Castleford by resting some players; he actually played Graeme West that day. We had 22,000 people there, on that Sunday. On the Tuesday it was Widnes, and they scored first through some brilliant rugby by Jonathon Davies. There were 28,000 people there to see us beat them 28–6. How John got them up for that game I will never know. So we had 50,000 spectators through the turnstiles in seventy-two hours!

On the Thursday we faced Bradford and were absolutely shattered. By the half-time break, we were 18 points to 2 down! In the half-time break John and Ellery raised the players' spirits so incredibly that they went out for the second half, and Kelvin Skerrett, along with Ellery, led the charge and they came back to get an 18–18 draw. We could have won the game but a late drop goal shaved the outside of the post!

In the match Andy Gregory damaged a hamstring, so could not play the next game two days later. John put young Bobby Goulding into the side! He actually won the man of the match against Leeds, but I do not know how we did it, and I don't think we could ever do it again. Against all the odds, we beat Leeds in thrilling style to lift the league trophy. We had seen 70,000 people come to Central Park in five days and no one gave us a prayer, especially in that last game at Leeds without 'Greg'. John Monie motivated the entire squad for the whole of that last incredible week. Without doubt that feat beat all the Wembleys, all the championships, all the eighty-minute specials. I do not think anyone else could have done what John Monie did.

So why was it that Hanley, such an inspirational captain, was allowed to leave the Wigan club?

John was not happy about that. As he told me, 'Where do you find champions like Ellery?' I explained to him, 'I have not sold Ellery to Leeds; Ellery has decided to go! We get £250,000 cash, which is not what I would have preferred, but if he intends to go we must make the best of it.' I promised John we would fix it. I brought in Billy McGinty from Warrington for £60,000 after Andy Gregory had recommended him to me. John said to me, 'You have bought a £60,000 player and sold the best player in the world for £250,000,' but, as I said, Ellery wanted to go and Billy would bring enthusiasm into the club. In the end John backed my judgement, and if you recall in 1992 the whole of the Wigan pack, including McGinty, represented Great Britain against Australia in Melbourne!

Whoever you talk to about Monie all say the same thing: he sees to the little things as well as the big things and it is that which brings success. Lindsay is no exception. When Monie approached him with the idea of bringing Bob Lanigan over to the club, there was no hesitation.

I had no problem with that, simply because John had assessed matters at the club first. He was not the sort of person to say on the phone 'I want to bring blokes with me.' He came and had a look first. We had a sprint coach whom Shaun Edwards had recommended, so I was thinking along those lines of having specialist coaches. When John brought Bob in, it was not to improve the athleticism of the team, but for power, as he was good on the weights. He transformed the gym into a heavy-metal room, and I do not mean music, and set up personal work cards for the players. John was the first one to do that in this country. He brought with him all the Parramatta standards and set them down at Central Park. That was the beginning of the Wigan '400 Club'. (To join, you needed to have bench pressed 400 lbs.) I had no hesitation simply because I knew we needed as many fresh ideas as possible over here if the club was to continue making progress.

It must be said that Lindsay was doing this at a time when 'greats' in the game, like Alex Murphy, were slamming any ideas which had any Australian connection, and the club was having great success.

When Lindsay left Wigan, he recalls the effect it had on his coach, who had come initially for two years and was to remain for four in deference to the chairman.

He was disappointed I was leaving, but I told him it was a chance to run the game as a whole and I felt I had to take the chance. He agreed, feeling the game needed someone to have a go at it. He did say to me on the day I left, 'I have to say that I do not think Jack Robinson is going to be able to handle this job.' He was very critical of Jack, as I am sure he would tell you himself, and he made a prediction: 'The foundation of the club is so strong, and the juniors coming through are so good, that the club will actually be stronger in the first year, but after that it will collapse.'

He was so right, and it was soon shown when Jack did

not re-sign Gene Miles. What a disgraceful decision that was: I was heartbroken. I had handed over the chairmanship and the first thing he did was sack Gene Miles, the local hero. I actually asked Jack why he had sacked him and his reply was that he thought he was getting a bit old! I tried to tell him that Gene was not old; he was a champion and he had played like a champion for us. Jack never liked Gene, but I also think it broke Martin Offiah's heart because Gene's last two games for us were the cup semi-final and final! Equally, in one game he had put Martin in for ten tries!

Perhaps the seeds in Robinson's mind were sown in the early part of Miles' season at Wigan following a quite remarkable episode, which also illustrates the world-wide support the club and Monie generated. As Lindsay explains:

I was actually in New York and flying back on Concorde. The captain was a Wigan fan, believe it or not, and I told him that we had a Lancashire Cup semi-final at St Helens that same evening. I had worked out that if I made the 6.30 p.m. shuttle from London up to Manchester I could get to the ground for the second half. The captain radioed ahead to Heathrow and arranged for me to get off Concorde first, had transport waiting to ferry me straight to the shuttle terminus and arranged for me to get away from Manchester airport. That was in the days when Concorde pilots had clout!

I duly got to Knowsley Road as the second half was just starting and asked how we were doing. It was Jack who answered. 'Badly,' he replied, 'and Gene Miles is playing like an old man.'

We found out that Gene had a tear in a thigh muscle but did not want to drop himself, thinking he would be letting everyone down. John Monie had talked with him but

> suggested I tried to persuade him to get the injury healed. I remember going to see Gene, who was embarrassed; I suspect thinking I was there to sack him. I wasn't. I simply told him to stop playing, get the injury right, come back and show everybody how good a player he really was. He did so, but in Jack's eyes I think he was still 'an old man'.
>
> For all the heartbreaking reasons, Monie's prediction was proved absolutely right. After the year was up, he rang to tell me he was not staying, feeling the club would crack. Once it became known he wished to go, he was approached by Auckland Warriors. Peter Mcleod rang me and I gave John a great reference and I helped John structure his contract with Auckland. He went and, sadly, all the predictions he made came true.
>
> John, as you know, came back a second time once the new management took over from Jack Robinson. He had a good first year, but, unfortunately, things did not work out, and he left just before I took over for a second time as chairman. I did seriously think about reversing the decision, but it would not have been right for him. It is a measure of the guy that he let me off the hook by telling me it would not be right. He felt it would be wrong for him, the fans and myself to come back.

All too often in sport of any kind we hear the cry, 'Will we ever see his like again?' Usually, though, it is in reference to the players. Not very often can such a statement be made of a coach. Lindsay has no doubts about Monie:

> Coaches with the completeness of John Monie only come along two or three times in a century. They tell me that Jim Sullivan had it and they tell me that Jack Gibson had it. They also say that Wayne Bennett has got it. John is in that mould. He has such a flexible mind and such calmness and the ability to get on with anybody anywhere.

He proved that when I recommended him to the BBC as an analyst when games were televised. He was incredibly good for them because he did not do all the ranting and raving we got at that time, all the embarrassing things. What he brought was an educated, reflective and studious approach. When a try was scored, instead of the daft comment like 'Hasn't he got a big pair of thighs?', it was, 'If you go back three or four plays you can see how this try was actually created.' He would then take the viewers through it step by step, telling them how a team had worked to make a try happen, or force an error, and the viewers enjoyed the game so much more because of him. With a good broadcasting voice and his calmness, he was brilliant for television. It also told everyone else in the game that we had an outstanding coach here at Wigan.

It must be said that Lindsay was able to shatter one myth about Monie! He is often referred to as the Iceman, someone who never loses his temper. Lindsay can remember one incident some time after he arrived at Central Park:

It was the semi-final of the John Player Cup at Headingley and we were playing Halifax. We were behind at half-time by a couple of points when John went in and scattered the teacups! He launched into them saying, 'I have been told you fellows have got this great desire to win Challenge Cups at Wembley but you cannot even win a semi in the John Player Cup. Don't talk to me about Wembley, which you have been doing since I arrived here, when you cannot apply your minds to winning this game.' In my experience it is the only time he has ever lost his temper, although it could have been contrived!

It was then the players realised that this quiet general was not having any nonsense. It was not that he did not have the ability to crack someone if needed. When he was a player, his brother told me all about him being called the 'Assassin' in the country league. When he first started, he used to smash people; opposition players were afraid of him! At Cronulla he played with Tommy Bishop, who was a fiery character also. He was a very powerful man and a great surfer. I think he was the under-21 national surfing champion in Australia. Consequently, he had such confidence in himself and, as a true man should have, he felt he did not need to prove anything. It is hard to imagine Monie, though, as an assassin, given his approach to the game today.

People talk of the success I have had; I could not have been successful without John Monie. He was, and is, a great coach, probably the greatest.

12

THOUGHTS OF DEAN BELL

During Monie's first spell in charge at Wigan he was blessed with two excellent captains. When he arrived he inherited Ellery Hanley, who at that time was considered to be the world's most outstanding player. He was an inspirational leader on the field and, contrary to popular belief, off it as well. It is well known that he had a run-in with certain members of the 'fourth estate', which resulted in him refusing to speak to journalists. Quite rightly a great many rugby league writers, who had done him no harm, were somewhat aggrieved to be tarred with the same brush. That should not be allowed to detract from his contribution to the Wigan cause.

Sadly, just as Monie's squad was at the height of its powers, Hanley decided to return to Leeds, which was after all his home-town club. Monie had not only to replace 'Hanley the player' but also 'Hanley the captain'. The former was done by allowing Phil Clarke to blossom as loose forward. It is well documented just how successful that move proved to be; the latter was done by giving the captaincy to New Zealand centre Dean Bell. It also was to prove an inspired choice. Bell, like his predecessor, was a captain who led from the front. Moreover, he proved himself to be the equal of Hanley as a leader on and off the field.

He was a different character from Hanley. Hanley was the artist, the pearl. If the job needed brute force, Ellery could do it. Equally, if the job needed guile then he could still finish the job. Bell was the enforcer. That is not to say he was lacking in skill; far from it. As a centre he was up there with the very best. No, what set Bell apart was his ability to carry on playing the game whatever the adversity. When it came to Wigan he was completely uncompromising; winning was what mattered and to do that every player had to give his all and more. Bell did it when fully fit, but, as Monie would testify, he would do it when less than fully fit as well. When he crossed the whitewash onto the pitch you knew that he was prepared to give everything he had, and then some, in trying to win the game. The fans loved him for it and were quick to christen him 'Mean Dean'; it was a term of endearment but it was also their way of describing his uncompromising style of play. Should retribution be needed during a game for misdemeanours, real or imagined, fans knew from where it would be forthcoming! Bell was, and still is, not one to be content with the soft option; there is only one way, the right way! He was the perfect captain, as his philosophy closely matched that of his coach. What Monie said and did in training during the week, Bell and his players did on the park on match days, usually as a result of Bell's prompting. Like his coach, he could handle being beaten by a better side, although even that hurt, but what he could not handle was players who had not given everything, even in a lost cause.

Strangely enough, it was Monie's predecessor, Graeme Lowe, who had brought Bell to the club in the 1987 season. As Bell recalls:

> Graeme Lowe was the coach at the time and I felt he was the only coach. Basically I followed him over to Wigan

from Australia. He was the catalyst for me coming, but I could see what the club was trying to do at that time. There was a lot of rebuilding going on and I just looked at the players they already had on board. I did have an offer from Leeds at the same time and even though it was for more money I could see myself winning more games at Wigan. That was the key for me. The talent the Wigan club had available at that time and obviously having Lowe as coach, as well, helped me make up my mind.

It seems that Bell was no sooner settled in at the club than Lowe was shipping out back down under. Bell, like everyone else at the club, was left to wonder who was going to take over. When the news broke that it was to be John Monie, the Parramatta coach, Bell, unlike many others, was not completely in the dark about just who was coming to the club.

I was aware of John, with him being the head coach at Parramatta at the time. I did follow the Aussie game very closely. I was looking forward to working with him. I had enjoyed the time working with Graeme and learned so much from him. I was a little wary of a new coach, as all players are; you did not know what he was going to be like. When he arrived he had a different way of coaching from Lowe. What I found with both of them was that there was no clear right or wrong approach; they both had different styles.

Graeme was more of a motivator; John was a deep thinker about the game. I knew very early on that I was going to get on with him because I had suffered a few injuries at the time he came. I came back from injury with the team going pretty well and started to play on the wing [Joe Lydon was playing centre at the time] because they did not want to change the team around. At John's first training session he asked me, 'What are they

> doing playing you on the wing?' I admit I did not like playing on the wing at that stage in my career; I saw myself as an out-and-out centre. It seemed he had the same idea, and I remember thinking to myself that for a first meeting with a new coach it had gone off in a very positive way. I was pleased to hear him say what he did, and our relationship was built on after that. That was the difference between the two coaches, John lived and breathed the game, it was something he did twenty-four hours a day, and he thought deeply about it.

Bell also found that Monie was a much more technical coach than his predecessor had been. He could motivate players but felt that motivation was more easily achieved if the players were well prepared for each game and knew what was expected of them during the game. As Bell put it:

> John worked a lot on team plays in training. We used to work a hell of a lot on team plays. It was obviously beneficial to the way we played the game. The other advantage was that if we ever had any injury problems, which obviously you do during any season, the players who came into the side knew exactly what was expected of them. It was bred into the players at the club. Also, you know, John had the respect of every player because of his great knowledge of the game. So he was never afraid to throw youngsters in. It was all about timing, too. He knew that youngsters would come in and have a couple of good games and then they seemed to tail off. He knew how to handle them well, and that is the key in any management job; the youngsters never seemed to resent dropping back into reserve grade.

People talk of Monie's ability to drop people from the side who were not playing well. That is one side of Monie that Bell fortunately never experienced first hand; it never happened to him. However he did see Monie in action when dropping other players from the team and thought everything was done in a very professional manner. If someone needed to be left out, there is no other way you can deal with it except to be straight with the player.

> John was always very straight with players. Everyone knew where they stood. He got on well with players; he got close but not too close. That was a sign of his professionalism. He was close to the players in a rugby league sense but socially he kept his distance. It was not until the latter part of my career that I got a little closer to him. That came simply from being together for so many years.

Monie has this reputation of being cool under pressure; he is nicknamed the Iceman by many Australian journalists. He is not known to lose his temper often. Bell, however, has seen the other side of Monie, albeit not very often. Bell has a theory as to why the nickname should have evolved. It could be because of Monie's seemingly unflappable nature, or total concentration on the job in hand, whether it is giving a half-time team talk, telling a player he will not be playing, or simply getting a message over in training. What is important is to get the message across clearly and concisely so that the player understands clearly what is expected of him. That is difficult to achieve if judgement is clouded by a fit of pique or temper.

> I have seen him lose his temper, not often, I must say. He did not need to, simply because of his relationship with and respect from the players. You knew when John meant business. People have different styles but it was never his way to lose his rag; he was cool and collected. Then again he never had to really as we seemed to do the business on the field for him pretty regularly. He was a good example

for me when I went into my coaching career. You do not overuse the actual shouting and bawling that should be done just for effect. If you did it all the time it would not have the results you want.

To have the respect of the players and know what you are talking about is the most important thing. If you know what you are talking about the players will trust you.

Unlike many others when faced with the question 'What was Monie's greatest achievement during that first spell at Wigan?', quite surprisingly Bell seems not to follow the well-trodden path.

It is something I have said to John. I would not like to single out any one thing in particular. My sign of a good coach is not someone who comes in and does it once, rather like a flash-in-the-pan approach, but someone who can consistently get the best out of his players. I said to him one time, over a drink when I was back here coaching Leeds and he came over to see me, 'Winning trophies is not the greatest sign of a coach; the greatest sign is a coach who is able to lift the players and consistently improve them, and win trophies along the way,' and that is what John Monie did.

Many people have said that anyone could have coached the Wigan side that John had. I don't go along with that, simply because there were so many different strong personalities within that side. If you put them all together, a psychologist would probably say you have got a recipe for disaster there! It takes a special quality to mix all those talents and John was able to do that.

We had so many different personalities; just two are Andy Gregory, who simply could not shut up, a really funny guy, and Joe Lydon, who had such a dry sense of humour. Really it is about letting the players express themselves, letting the different personalities come out,

> but not letting them take over or shift the focus from the job in hand. At the end of the day, what made that Wigan side so successful, with the greatest respect to John and Graeme Lowe, was that the individuals they had under them were winners. They hated losing more than they liked winning: it was like that. It was a unique time of getting all those people together and may never happen again. But you need someone to steer the boat. John did a terrific job in doing just that.

Another quality Bell highlighted was Monie's ability to keep both the players and the team progressing. The club had a sprint coach, Bill Hartley, and the coming of Bob Lanigan to improve the power of players was seen by Bell as just another progression designed to maintain the edge that Wigan needed to continue winning games.

> We enjoyed having that edge on opponents. We were probably the first team to go full time. But that was mainly because we were winning our games. The players were not on huge salaries in the beginning, but they could afford to live on the winning money. We were not doing anything spectacular, but John was always looking for that edge. He actually introduced me to a lot of books. He gave me one, which even now I call my bible, which is called *The Winning Edge*. It has a lot of quotes and philosophies from a lot of famous sportspeople. He gave it to me in my last year at Wigan. It is something which means so much to me and I use it even to this day.

The Wigan team of the 1990s, when one looks back, suggests that it picked itself. It is easy to forget that one of Monie's skills was being able to pick teams to do particular jobs. It is a fact not lost on Bell, however, who pointed out that a great deal of the time the dilemma was really who to leave out of the side. He felt there were quite a number of combinations that one could come up with for the Wigan team of those successful years: 'John was also very good at looking ahead and knowing what we were coming up against, so he was able to select the best team for the job which needed to be done.'

Dean Bell was probably the most successful Wigan captain of any era. Sadly, it counted for little when Monie left the club to begin life as coach at Auckland. He, along with Monie, was targeted by the then chairman Jack Robinson. Bell is under no illusions about what went on at that period. The heady days of the end of his playing career at the club, the night Michael Aspel trod the hallowed turf at Central Park to say those world-famous words, 'Dean Bell, this is your life!'; all was forgotten as the fires were stoked by the press about Dean's desertion. How he was letting the club down and letting the fans down. Nothing could be further from the truth, as Bell explained:

> Most people would have done what John did in his position. He wanted to be successful, and he was successful at Wigan with certain players so he wanted to take those players. He knew what they could offer a new side like Auckland. You need good role models, so he took them with him. He certainly did not take me away from the Wigan club, because the club were not going to offer me a contract for the following year; Jack Robinson had told me so. I was all ready for retirement at the end of my contract.

It was a sad end to a career which had been of the highest quality. Wembley had become almost an annual event for Bell; cup and league doubles commonplace. Yet now he was being branded in some quarters as a traitor. Nothing could have been further from the truth, and the press coverage must have hurt Bell greatly. However, as in his playing career, he never let the opposition see he was hurting, so the Wigan public never got the real story.

It was inevitable that a Kiwi would want to return home and be part of the first New Zealand club side to play in the ARL. Bell could not resist the lure.

> You always want to do that! It would be nice to prove to people back home that you could do it. I had my doubts, though, mainly due to all the injuries I'd had. Would I still be able to do it in that competition? Having played there for three years I knew how tough it was. Coming up to thirty-three years of age and going back to that competition was a big thing to ask. John gave me the nudge. When he first said he wanted me to go back and captain the Warriors, I thought he was joking. I soon found out he was deadly serious and he convinced me!
>
> If it had not been for him; if he had not been the coach, I wouldn't have gone. That was the respect I had for him.

Bell, like Monie, became part of a brand-new club. He helped to mould the Auckland Warriors into a more than useful outfit. However, little credit was given to the efforts of the club. It must be said that the situation has not changed even today. The Kiwi media were used to success on the rugby field, to them rugby was union. They could not accept that in league it was the Aussies who were top dog. It did not sit well with them and they seemed to vent their spleen on the Warriors.

Bell, however, is in no doubt about just how successful the club was during that inaugural season.

> I thought we had a brilliant season, better and sooner than a lot of people would have imagined. There was so much pressure on the Warriors due to the hype. It was a fantastic year and a fantastic achievement.
>
> I think everyone involved with the club did the best job they could in that first season. John said thanks to

me in my last game at Erickson stadium in New Zealand. What he did not tell me was that he had arranged for the players to form a guard of honour onto the field for me. Later, John said it was one of the most emotional times in his career. It certainly was for me. Now, being a coach, I know just how he felt, because he'd had such a big influence on my career. I realise that I can have that influence on others. Bowing out as I did that last year in Auckland could not have been scripted better by anyone else! I was very pleased John had convinced me to go. As I say, I had my doubts at the start but hopefully repaid the faith John had had in me.

I felt we had a fantastic year. People forget that the players had never been exposed to the kind of intensity they got in the Aussie competition. We did better than I expected because, as I said earlier, John could get the best out of players for longer and with greater consistency than any other coach.

If I had to say what his greatest achievement was I suppose I would have to say it was when I wasn't at Wigan, when John came back the second time. He got them to lift the Super League trophy. I thought that was a tremendous achievement. The club had been fairly average by their standards up until then. He lifted them! Wigan will always have a team that can do it on the day, but John got them to lift the trophy. He did it by getting players to give him their best, week in week out, when they were fit and when they were carrying injuries! I do not know if winning that first Super League trophy was his greatest achievement, but it is certainly one that stood out for me.

Ironically, Bell is now back at Wigan as assistant to Frank Endacott and is also in charge of youth development. He is putting into practice the lessons learned from the master coach Monie, simply getting players to perform as well as they can, week after week.

13

THE TEAMS

'The team can do more than the individual can.'

John Monie has coached at the top level for twenty years or so. What makes him unique is that he has done so, not in one country, which in itself would be an achievement, but in three: Parramatta, in Australia; Wigan, in the UK; Auckland Warriors, in New Zealand; and the London Broncos, also in the UK. It is inevitable, when a coach has done all this, that many great players will have played for him. It is equally true that the questions that most fans want answering are: who was the best player you coached and which was the best team you coached?

These are questions which really are almost impossible for any coach to answer, particularly for someone like Monie, who has coached for such a long time. The game changes from one generation to another, and tactics change, as do players. It is notoriously difficult to take a player from one era and ask how he would perform in a different one. When you have coached over such a long period, it becomes very difficult to select teams, or individual players. The problem is that you cross eras, as well as countries. The style of play in England and Australia now is very different from that of the early 1980s, just as the style of the early 1990s differs from today's game. In an attempt to answer the fans' questions, Monie tried to stay within not only an era but also a country. To do so, he concentrated on selecting the best hypothetical Wigan side that he coached from the 1990s, and the best Parramatta side of the 1980s. The results are certain to get readers talking, not for the players who made the teams but perhaps for those who did not.

> I found it a difficult job to actually put down on paper the best sides I have coached. I would say some players, great players, would miss out on selection not because they weren't good enough, but because the qualities they had might not fit the 'team' requirement I was trying to achieve.
>
> The best Wigan team I have coached would be: full-back Radlinski, wings Martin Offiah and Jason Robinson, the centres would be Gene Miles and Dean Bell, the halfs Shaun Edwards and Andy Gregory, the props Kelvin Skerrett and Andy Platt with Martin Dermot at hooker. The second rows would be Andy Goodway and Andy Farrell, locking the pack would be Ellery Hanley. My bench players would be Andrew Farrar, Joe Lydon, Dennis Betts and Neil Cowie.
>
> Looking at the players individually, I went for Chris Radlinski over Steve Hampson because I felt he was a more complete player. Radlinski was just as good a competitor, but was more disciplined, although there was not a great deal between the two.
>
> Martin Offiah was just a phenomenal try-scorer. He could get across the line. He was the fastest player I have ever seen when he was in his prime; he understood the game and he took it very seriously. Everybody just saw him as a speed merchant, but he had a lot more to offer than that. Defensively, if he missed you the first time he

could pick you up a second time or even on the third attempt. After I had been coaching him for a while, I didn't have a lot of complaints about his defence; he gave players the outside and could always run them into the side line. He stopped them, but this wasn't his strong point: it was his speed and getting across the line which he turned into an art form.

On the other wing, Jason Robinson was a totally different character: a very hard worker and dummy-half runner extraordinaire. He would run from dummy half and pick up more yards down the middle than any forward in the game, then he could also finish on the wing for you. He could score a long-range try as well. Defensively, he tackled very well; he was just a little vulnerable on the cross-field kicks into the corners because of his size.

In the centres we had big, tough, rough guys who could play football; no one went past them. Gene Miles was a basketball player playing rugby league with great hands. Because he was so big with such good ball skills he must have been a dream to play outside of, or inside of, for that matter. The way he could get passes away after committing two or three defenders was just unbelievable. He was pretty tough in defence, a good hitter.

When I first got to Wigan, Dean Bell needed to become more disciplined. Once that was in control, he turned out to be a great, uncompromising leader. He would knock you down and keep you down. Defensively there was no one better. He was, I think, in the Andrew Farrar mould: knock 'em down, drag 'em out style! And he could run in a try from fifty metres. His hands were not Gene Miles' hands, but they were pretty good. He was a good player in attack but defence was his strong point.

It was an ideal combination in the centres. As a coach, it is important to be able to select ideal combinations, to be able to select a team. Maurice Lindsay always said that a lot of coaches he had worked with did not have the ability to select the right teams. One of my strengths has always been the ability to pick a team and make sure the combinations were right. With Miles and Bell you could not ask for anything better if you were playing inside or outside those two.

At half we had Shaun Edwards, who was tactically very aware, set up his supports well and understood the game. One of his strengths was the ability to put players into holes and support. The team always had good service from him, and [Andy] Gregory. He was brave and went above the call of duty on many occasions, Warrington at Wembley being one which comes to mind. He fractured an eye socket, saw the game out and we dropped him off at the hospital on the way to the celebrations!

Like Edwards, Gregory was another 'one-off', so well suited to the English game. He was a character, he was tough, he could put the ball where a player had to run on to, and if the receiver's timing was good he would run into a hole nine times out of ten. Not only did he know where to put the ball, he demanded to be given ball from dummy half. If Gregory was playing half-back and there was a back-line shot on, he got the ball. There were no missed calls, or dummy half saying, 'I didn't know Andy Gregory wanted the ball.' His presence was such that when he wanted it, he demanded it, and he got it! A lot of half-backs will tell you they get the ball one ruck too late, but every time Andy Gregory saw something on, he had the presence and he got the ball. You wouldn't say either he or Edwards was strong defensively. They had been brought up in the English game as 'footballers', as the Aussies would say. Defence was not a priority with them. They could defend but it was not their strong point, they were about getting the football in their hands and doing something with it. Gregory would run at the defensive line many a time and as he was built like a pocket battleship, it would be all action!

The front row I have selected was quite a formidable unit. Kelvin Skerrett was the intimidator, a very tough man although, like all tough guys, he sometimes overplayed his hand and had to pay the price. He could get the ball forward, and pick up yards even in the tightest games. Defensively, other people would tread lightly when Kelvin was in the vicinity. He was a good, no-nonsense, front-row player, and even if he did overstep the mark, you have to have a little bit of that in your football team!

On the other side was Andy Platt: Mr Consistency, Mr Toughness. He would be unlucky to be penalised, but he was there to take the ball up whenever the hard stuff was on. He was there to dish it out, too, when the opposition were trying to come up the middle. Superbly conditioned and mentally very tough, he trained himself into being just a great front-row forward. He also had a pass in him, as did Kelvin, so it was not just power.

The hooker Martin Dermot was a fantastic dummy half. Every ball came off the ground in a split second and was right where Andy Gregory wanted it – most of the time. He was an aggressive player, with good speed when he decided to take off out of dummy half. He had vision, but he knew if 'Greg' at half-back didn't want the ball, then he was working the forwards. He and Gregory kept it like that; pretty simple but effective.

The second row of [Andy] Goodway and [Andy] Farrell was another good combination. The selection of Andy Goodway may well raise an eyebrow or two, but he was probably one of the best running back-row forwards I have ever coached. With a guy like Gregory in your football team, to put the ball into space, Goodway would always run into a hole. That is something which is very difficult to coach a player to do. Andy Goodway was as good at hitting gaps as any player I have ever seen, with strength, speed and versatility. I played him in the front row, the second row, loose forward, centre and even on the wing when we had an injury. He had speed which was good enough to allow him to play on the inside of one of those centres of ours.

Andy Farrell was big! People don't realise how big he is! He has the skills of a half-back, the hands of a stand-off, and with good ball vision produced a great kicking game. With Edwards, Gregory and Farrell in the side, your kicking game was covered. Farrell could always get a ball away in traffic. He was a very talented player who complemented Goodway's skills.

Behind the pack was Ellery Hanley: the complete player. He was a great captain; he led the way at training and could talk tough to the players when they needed it. When he got on the football field he was able to defend very well but was able to play attacking rugby league either tight as a front rower or looser in the back row, or very loose as a centre. He had qualities which could get the ball from our try-line to our twenty-metre line. He would take the ball up nice and tight for you and absorb whatever was coming. When we got down to the other end of the field and were shifting the ball out, he had the qualities to get out there and beat people out wide. He was deceptively quick, and very quick going sideways as well. He used to twist away from people or push away from them and be almost running in a sideways motion. He also knew where the try-line was! If there was a try to be scored, and it looked to me from the side line there was half a chance if Ellery got the ball, he would get over the line.

My bench players were selected to complement and replace team members. First, I would have Andrew Farrar, a tough, uncompromising centre. I coached him for just the one season, but by halfway through that season he was starting to use the ball as the English game required centres to use the ball. He did not have a lot of that in him when he started playing for us; he was a bit head down, backside up, just advancing the ball and playing it back fast. That was what playing in Sydney had taught him; at Wigan he started to come out of his shell with the ball in his hands. He became a good all-round player; his strongest point though was being very tough in defence. If you had to lose one of your centres then you would not miss much with Farrar stepping onto the park.

The other back on the bench was Joe Lydon, a very, very talented man, but not the hardest trainer in the world. He kicked the ball fantastically well, but give him just a little bit of room to move and he could beat the opposition. Defensively, he had enough talent to get by. He had a massive kick on him which was a strength. Again, if you had to pull Miles and Bell out you lost very little by putting Farrar and Lydon in.

Dennis Betts is one of the greatest professionals I have ever worked with; he made himself good. He is a big man who could run the football, he could play in the centres, he could play in the back row. He has made himself what he is and that is what I admire most about him. In a way he was an Andy Goodway protégé. Andy had a good bit to do with moulding him and forming his attitude, and Dennis learned his lessons well. It would be hard for me to pick a football team now without putting Dennis Betts in. I have tremendous admiration for him and what he has done in the game.

Finally, Neil Cowie. Again, I think his selection may also raise an eyebrow or two; prop is a tough position to play and he is a very awkward player to tackle. He gets his low centre of gravity to work, he leans forward a long way on contact but is always prepared to pull the ball back and get an off-load. In the modern game the way it is played now most teams have to have a front-rower like Cowie who can get the ball away. He is uncompromising and aggressive in defence, which you needed. I would not like to have him and Kelvin Skerrett in the same front row; you might be in trouble as far as the penalties went. But if Kelvin had to come off in a game and Cowie went on, then I would feel very comfortable about it.

When you go through the seventeen players you could say that individually they were characters. They all had funny traits or peculiar ways – with Skerrett and Cowie there was a bit of devil; a bit of mischief. Andy Platt – you were always having a good time if Andy was around. Gregory and Edwards were a little different; they all had that little something I could not coach.

When I started to look at the best Parramatta team it was a little more difficult, simply because I had to get into the mood of the game back in the '80s. So I had to judge players against the standards of their generation rather than against the standards of today's game and its different demands. I did, however, come up with a formidable team: full-back Paul Taylor, wings Neil Hunt and Eric Grothe, centres Steve Ella and Mick Cronin, halfs Brett Kenny and Peter Sterling, props Geoff Bugden and Paul Mares with Stephen Edge at hooker, second rows Steve Sharp and Peter Wynn, locking the pack Ray Price. On the bench would be Mark Laurie, Bob Lindner, John Muggleton and Michael Erikson.

Paul Taylor at full-back was a workaholic, who would move into the front line when there was tackling to be done because Sterling had dropped back to have a little bit of a break. He was not the biggest, built more like a half-back, but he was so good a footballer we had to get him into the side somewhere. He could play first receiver or half-back when we had the football in attacking positions. All in all he was a great trainer, with a bit of devil in him, a little wild off the field but a good guy to be around.

On one wing, Neil Hunt represented New South Wales in the State of Origin series; good finisher. Jack Gibson nicknamed him 'Guilty' because he felt everytime he looked at him, Neil had a guilty look on his face! So 'Guilty' stuck. He could get across the line and had good handling skills, which meant he did not drop anything. On the other wing we had Eric Grothe, Mr Explosion. If he could not go round them he would go through them! He had similar explosive qualities to Jason Robinson, but Eric was twice as big as Jason. He terrorised English teams when he came on the tours. You did not need to give him any room because he would just go through you anyway. But he was never going to improve the position for the kicker because once he saw the try-line he put the ball down.

In the centre was 'Zip', Stevie Ella. Where Grothe was a power runner, Steve was a player who floated across the ground: a beautiful, effortless runner. We used to double the centres up a lot more in those days [whereas today we tend to split them on each side of the field] so 'Zip' could run onto some beautiful balls from Mick Cronin.

Cronin, 'The Crow', had hands like Andy Farrell, and could stand up strongly in the tackle, and while having the attention of two or three tacklers, still off-load the ball. He could run into a hole very well but was very stiff in the back! We always laughed about him not being able to bend over well. For his time, he was the greatest centre in world rugby and was a phenomenal goal-kicker – an unbelievable goal-kicker.

If the half-backs I had at Wigan were suited to the English game, the half-backs at Parramatta were suited to any game, anywhere. You would have to come up with a very special couple to beat Kenny and Stirling.

Brett Kenny was the most talented back-line player I have ever coached! With great vision, he was very relaxed and just did everything so effortlessly. Defensively, he was very good, but with his change of pace and his side step and swerve he was a dream player. I don't think he even got excited when he played at Wembley for Wigan in 1985–86. He was the most gifted rugby league player I have ever seen.

Peter Sterling, inside Kenny, was the coach on the field. He had a great understanding of the game and was able to put into practice what he had learnt during the week, even under game pressure. The bigger the game, the more pressure on him, the better Peter Sterling played.

One prop was Geoff Bugden, probably a bigger version of Andy Platt, with a lot of the same attributes as Platt. He was very disciplined; never gave away many penalties.

Paul Mares had his career cut short by recurring knee injuries and was finished before he was twenty-five, but he had great talent. He was a very big front-rower but could run like a back-rower, with phenomenal pace and agility. He was very aggressive; even our own players at team meetings used to complain they had been smacked by Paul Mares in the tackle! He had great enthusiasm to get into the tackle, be it second, third, or even fourth man! He had good hands, but then he was like a back-rower playing front row.

Stephen Edge was my hooker and I would think he captained more sides (if not the top he was certainly in the top three) to win grand finals in Australia than any other player. I think he had a couple at St George, then he captained Parramatta to three, and was my captain in 1984. Steve was just one of the older-style hookers: not the sharpest out of dummy half, nor the quickest player over twenty metres. He just had success wherever he went and it was mainly through his mental toughness and his desire to get the job done without deviating from the game plan. Once he had confidence in something, Stephen Edge would carry it out to the letter, and everywhere he played he got results! A very tough guy, but a good guy, whose team-mates regarded him highly and believed in him. He was a great captain; players followed him. He said it and they all did it! It was a great skill to have.

Of the two second-row men, Stephen Sharp scored the first-ever try at the new Parramatta stadium. He was an uncompromising player, a tough defender and would just keep taking the ball up for the team. He had a pass in him, had a bit of football in him, and when I look back through all the good sides Parramatta had over those years, Stephen Sharp's name keeps coming up in them. He wasn't in the Australian side or anything like that, but for Parramatta his name was there week in and week out. He rarely missed a game! Mr Dependable.

The other second row was Peter Wynn, a tall gangly player who could make a break and run the football. When you look at the Parramatta sides of the '80s they were all hard workers and Wynn was just that. Many did not get representative honours, particularly the forwards, but when you look at the half-backs you can see our forwards had a job to do: driving the ball up to an attacking position, then letting Kenny and Sterling go to work.

At loose forward we had Ray Price, Mr Perpetual Motion, 'never say die'; you could knock him down, carry him off on a stretcher and he would wake up and come running back on! He was great, he was obnoxious, a pain in the opposition's backside and a pain to the referees as well. Whilst very aggressive, always in your face, and not always pretty, he simply wanted to get the job done. If he could get it done and spill a little blood, then he was even happier.

On the bench I had Mark Laurie; his nickname was 'Pebbles' because his brother, who had won a Rothman's medal in Sydney playing for Eastern Suburbs, was 'Rocky' Laurie. He was a good loose forward, with a good step, who had played a bit of football in England, which had suited him. He was a good ball handler, a typical back-row player who was also good defensively.

When Ray Price retired, we brought Bob Lindner to the club to try and take over the loose-forward role. He didn't really settle in Sydney, being a Queenslander, and didn't stay long at the club. I felt he had a very good season in 1987 and gave his best every week, but it was unfortunate he didn't settle to the Sydney lifestyle.

John Muggleton was a centre with Parramatta and Jack Gibson was looking for a running back-row forward who could do something with the football, We decided we would take John Muggleton from the centres in the second grade and start to play him in the back-row. It was my job to try and turn him into a back-row forward. By the end of the season he was getting into Jack Gibson's side as a back-rower; he also got selected to play for Australia in the same position. I felt I did a pretty good job with him!

Last of all, Michael Erikson, again a pretty big kid from the country who we signed from Taree. When Michael Cronin retired, we had the idea to play Michael in the centre, and he played a lot of his games for Parramatta either in the centre or on the wing. He had good speed but not particularly good hands. Because we had brought him in to replace 'The Crow', the players nicknamed him 'The Sparrow'.

Like the Wigan team, this Parramatta side were a team

with lots of character. Michael Cronin was Mr Nice Guy. Steve Ella and Brett Kenny were very relaxed. Eric Grothe had his strange ways. If you looked at the pack you would have to say there was more talent in the back row of the Wigan pack, but that, I feel, just highlights the difference between the game in Sydney and the game in England.

Having selected the two teams, I felt that there were other players who were so close I would look at a third team, who were the players who didn't quite make my first selections. At full-back I would choose Steve Hampson, the wings were Frano Botica and John Kerwin; in the centre Kevin Iro and Gary Connelly; the halfs were Greg Alexander at stand-off and Stacy Jones inside him; the front row of Joe Vagana, Robbie McCormack and Les Davidson; second row would be Simon Haughton and Stephen Kearney; with Philip Clarke at the back of the scrum. On the bench Mark Bell, Henry Paul, Justin Dooley and Billy McGinty.

It was a toss-up between Billy and Mick Cassidy but in the end Billy got the nod.

Steve 'Hampo' at the back was dependable, did not make many mistakes, was great under the high ball and played the game with a twinkle in his eye; bit of a lad!

Botica developed into a better player than ever I thought he could. He had good skills and was a former All Black who sat behind Grant Fox in that great side they had. He could play stand-off or scrum-half, as well as full-back and wing. He turned out to be a phenomenal goal-kicker for Wigan, and he was great to coach. John Kerwin, the ex-All Black we drafted into the Auckland side, was included simply because he knew how to win. He knew what it took, knew a lot about preparation and probably his best days were behind him when he was on the wing for Auckland. He still turned out to be our top try-scorer, so he could get across the line. Again, he was very knowledgeable and fun to be around.

In the centre was Kevin Iro, a try-scorer in big games. That is all I have to say about him; you get into a big game, Kevin will score you tries. In 1998 at Wigan, Connelly showed himself to be the best centre in the league in England. Nobody beat him. He had problems with his knee, so when he could train, he always gave his best. On match days he could knock 'em down when they had the football, and when he got it he could do something good with it.

Henry Paul was an individualist, playing a lot for himself, but he was a winner. He was not as disciplined as I would have hoped, but had great talent. Stacy Jones, what can I say? I brought Greg Alexander to Auckland to play half-back and Stacy was so good that half-way through the season I moved Greg to full-back so I could play Stacy. He had the head of a very experienced half-back on his shoulders when he was seventeen or eighteen years old. His short kicking game was good, and he could attack the line with the ball in his hand.

One of the two props was Joe Vagana, a Polynesian who was big and raw; a huge player. He enjoyed the physical contact of running into people; defensively he would smash people. He had a good pass as well. On the other side was Les Davidson, who came to Wigan and played for ten weeks. Again a very aggressive player but with a pass in him; he was tough and uncompromising in his approach to the game.

Stephen Kearney was a talented player who could pass the football in the tightest of situations. Defensively, he was aggressive and got into hot water with the referees, so he did not miss them when he had to do some tackling. Simon Haughton was a fast power runner, and in a big game he would always make a break for me. I love the players who can do that little bit more. He wasn't a great defender or a hurtful defender but he could get the job done. When we had the football in big games, he could get across the line; he scored tries in big games, and I like that in a back rower.

Philip Clarke, at loose forward, probably thought a little too much about the game. Mentally he was a little bit complicated, and wanted everything in place. He could run the ball, understood the game, and was an intelligent player. He was not your blood and guts type of player, unlike Hanley, who could play it whichever way it had to be played, and Ray Price, who wasn't happy until he had seen a little blood. Philip was not in that style, though fundamentally he was very good; his speed was good, and he had a pass in him, and did the right things when he had to.

On the bench was Mark Bell, who played for the 1998 Wigan grand final side. He had a great desire to score tries, and was well schooled in the game. Whoever coached him early in his career should get a lot of credit. He was always where a winger should be; when you watched him play from the stand he was always in the right place. A great competitor! Greg Alexander was another talented, talented player. Penrith was his club; he was only at Auckland a couple of seasons. When he got on the park he could play the game. He had his problems off the field but come three o'clock on Sunday afternoon you were a lucky coach if you had Greg in your team.

Justin Dooley and Billy McGinty just had a great desire to be successful. Billy was like a bit player, not one of the stars. He wasn't the guy who won the big game, but you were never going to lose a game because of Billy. Justin had all the qualities of a front-rower: hard nosed, aggressive, a great off-loader under pressure.

That team could hold its own in the highest company, I would think.

The other point that needs to be made, I think, is one that struck me as I drew up my best Wigan side and my best Parramatta side. Both teams had one thing in common, and that was that they stayed together as teams! They stayed together right the way through the successful periods. In Sydney, Parramatta were always being poached by other clubs. The players all had offers to leave and they all stayed. In Wigan, players did not want to leave and that loyalty to 'the team' was the one constant in both clubs. No one got the disease of 'more' because they wanted more money, more status etc., they all stayed. Probably it was because they all liked each other and they all played the game with smiles on their faces and twinkles in their eyes!

One of the questions supporters ask me quite a lot is, 'Who was the best player you ever coached?' There is no doubt in my mind it was Brett Kenny; if I had to pick an English player it would be Ellery Hanley, but Kenny was the best I ever coached.

I would not want people to think that other coaches and I got it right all the time. As I said earlier, there were times when I disagreed with Maurice Lindsay at Wigan, and also with Ian Robson at Auckland. I respected their sporting knowledge enough to be able to sit down with them and resolve the differences we had; sometimes I won, sometimes I lost. It was the same with players; sometimes I got the best out of them, sometimes I didn't. Henderson Gill at Wigan was a case in point. When I got to Wigan, Henderson blew his chances; I know he was coming to the end of his career but I had seen him do such great things. It must have been in 1989–90, when he was not turning up for training, or was late for training sessions, so half-way through the year I cut him.

> It is always tough when you have to make those sorts of decisions. Maybe Henderson had done enough, and had had enough by then, and wanted to quit.

As Monie heads for home and the surf starts to look more and more attractive, I wonder if he feels he has had enough, has done enough. It would be a great loss to the game of rugby league if he does.

EPILOGUE

John Monie's bare feet had hardly touched the sand, or his surfboard, at his new headquarters on Queensland's Sunshine Coast before he was off to Papua New Guinea to help the locals take on a visiting French team over two Tests.

> The local New Guineans love their rugby league as much or even more than anyone in the game and show it by flooding the grounds with, say, 10,000 inside and 20,000 outside trying to get in!
>
> I'd arrived at very short notice, three days in fact, after a call from Papua New Guinea coach Bob Bennett, the brother of Bronco and Queensland coach Wayne. The locals weren't allowed to bolster their national team with their internationals, like the Storm's Marcus Bal or Wigan's Adrian Lam, and they were a bit short on the ground as far as experience was concerned.
>
> Their team was made up of locals and some players from the Queensland Cup, but what they lacked in experience they made up with the fire in their bellies. The French must

have wondered what they'd struck when they ran out on that steamy night to be greeted by wave upon wave of whistling, brawling enthusiasts trying to break down the gates into the stadium.

I was doing a broadcast from the roof and had a bird's-eye view as police poured tear-gas into the crowds. It brought back memories from Wigan days when the touring Great Britain side visited New Guinea and Martin Dermott and Denis Betts came home with stories about the clash and the crowds and the very real feeling they weren't going to get out of New Guinea alive!

John experienced this for himself when he was on a day's break between the two Test matches. The man who held the Nike franchise in the country invited John for a round of golf. John was picked up from the hotel and as they drove to the course they passed Parliament House and saw a huge protest in progress which caused some alarm. As John arrived at the golf club he was met by a security guard armed with a machine-gun who inquired, 'Are you John Monie?' Having established his identity, John was informed that the security guard was 'going to protect you from the rascals' while he played his round of golf. John and his host then made their way to the first tee where two native tribesmen were waiting – armed with bows and arrows! As Monie remarked to his host: 'A little bit different from the calm surroundings I am used to at Pelican Waters Golf Club.'

PNG lost the first Test at Port Moresby, but with a bit more time to coach them I went with the team to Goroka in the Highlands and we scored a rare victory. This team of no stars was fast running out of steam towards the end of the game, but they bravely held on for a 32–27 victory. There was near pandemonium at the end, but it was just great to see the joy of success on their faces.

Papua New Guineans will always be up against it trying

> to beat visiting Test teams. There's nothing wrong with their tickers and they get teak-tough with the right training and coaching, but they don't grow tall enough to match it with 6ft-plus visitors and, of course, they need lots more regular competition. Both Lam, the former Roosters and Wigan player and Queensland skipper, and Bal, the Storm flyer, have shown what can be achieved under the right conditions.
>
> Sadly, the PNG competition had to be scrapped in 2002 due to the local elections. It's understandable, though, when we're told there were at least four shot dead in Mt Hagen, dozens were injured, a reporter was chased and stoned, while some militia threatened to shoot down any aircraft that tried to land to pick up ballot boxes!

Monie and his family planned their move to Queensland's Sunshine Coast with the same meticulous care that the super coach had brought home six league championships with by the time he was 52, making him the first coach to guide teams to Grand Final wins on both sides of the world.

The Monies were living in Auckland where John coached the Warriors. They had decided several years before they wanted to spend the rest of their lives in the sun after some freezing winters in Britain and wet ones in New Zealand, so Julie Monie went scouting. She ended up at a new development called Pelican Waters in Caloundra on the Sunshine Coast and there bought a waterside block where the Monie home was built.

Now, with 18 months of surfing, crabbing and golf under his belt, the coach is cautiously seeking new fields to conquer. But, as he puts it, there are less than 30 top league clubs here and overseas so the job market is pretty cramped for someone whose career has been rugby league for four decades.

> I'm not holding my breath and I'd find it pretty tough having to leave the coast. There are very few places where

> the sun shines most of the year; where the crabs are always there in season; where the surf runs almost every day; the tennis court is across the road and the golf club is within walking distance of our home.

Not long after his return home, Monie was asked to become a mentor coach for Queensland's up-and-coming youngsters who are offered scholarships at Canberra's élite Australian Institute of Sport (AIS). The Canberra set-up follows on the heels of Queensland's institute developed by master coach and Monie's friend Wayne Bennett. Monie travels around Queensland checking juniors from 13 years upwards to scholarship level, which starts at 17. Queensland has 15 of the 35 teenagers at the Canberra AIS, a big compliment to those who had the foresight to get it underway. Most of the players on the two-year scholarship are supported by or contracted to NRL clubs.

> It's not before time we've got élite youngsters coming through the system like this,' says Monie. 'But there are some facets of the system which may get out of hand if we don't keep a tight rein. For instance, I was recently in Townsville at the Junior Rugby League State Championships for under-13, 14 and 16 year olds. Also there were club scout representatives like the great Artie Beetson for the Roosters and Noel Cleal for Parramatta. These former top players have been responsible for bringing on dozens of kids over the years. However, a worrying aspect for me was that freelance player agents were not only there looking at signing on older kids, they were also assessing the under-13s. So much so a youngster I spoke to said he wasn't allowed to say anything without his agent present!
>
> These are kids hardly out of primary school and I reckon they should be let alone to get on with their enjoyment of the game and their school work for at least a few years

longer. A lot of the kids who come to the junior championships are accompanied by their mums, who can be easy meat for the sweet-talking new breed of agent who may promise a lot to try and sign promising kids. Perhaps agents should be kept on hold at least until the kids have turned 16.

Most of the kids getting a chance at the Canberra AIS scholarships are from country centres, the breeding ground for many of Australia's great rugby league players. There's not much chance of a kid getting noticed somewhere like Cunnamulla if he can't get to a country centre where his wares can be scrutinised. Kids shouldn't be disadvantaged just because of where they live so the more times we can push into the bush the better as far as I'm concerned.

Monie 'The Iceman', the coachs' coach, who once hated reading the newspapers after a game, has made a successful switch to author and columnist, and weekly registers his feelings about the game he loves and the people involved in it. He doesn't pull any punches when he says there should immediately be a fighting fund set up under an independent committee by the CEO of the NRL to battle the theft of top league players by rugby union.

The fans go along to games to see their team and particularly the stars. You can't blame people who get frustrated after a club has brought along young Billy from his teens to the big time, formed their own cheer squad around him, got his autograph a dozen times and then found he's buzzed off to another game for more money than league can afford to pay him. You can't blame the player; there aren't that many years where the body can take the big punishment at the top, so he has to make the most of what's on offer. Surely the NRL can come up with something to counter the problem. Another blight on the Australian game is the mid-season anti-tampering deadline on 30 June. This should immediately be shifted to midnight on the day of the Grand Final and all the pressure taken off the players, clubs and, even more importantly, the fans.

Monie believes the days of the 'hit run' Test series should be ended after the fiasco of Great Britain's worst-ever thumping by the Aussies on Bleak Friday, 12 July 2002.

You don't have to cast your mind back far to recall that on the last Australian visit to England the Kangaroos were whacked in the first Test under similar circumstances – a short work-up and into it. After settling down the Kangaroos went on to win the series and perhaps there would have been a closer contest here had there been more time for acclimatisation.

It may have been closer over three Tests, but I reckon the English representative standards are being affected by Aussie and Kiwis playing there, keeping local talent from progressing.

International rugby league should not become a mockery. There doesn't seem much point in throwing on Tests if there is no test for Australia. The only country within coo-ee of the Aussies is New Zealand and that's because the Warriors are competition hardened and come ready to play, and because of the number of Kiwis and Pacific Islanders (who can also front up for NZ) playing in the NRL competition for almost every club.

The Kangaroos played superbly against Great Britain, but I believe a lot of fans will have gone away shaking their heads about the display from the opposition. As a coach in England for years, I believe there has got to be a better way of structuring representative football for the fans who cough up lots to see their heroes go round. Perhaps we should concentrate more on a tri series between Australia,

New Zealand and Great Britain, playing home and away.

I understand how important it is and how proudly rugby league players wear the green and gold, but if there's no one left standing to play against it's pointless.

Australia had a strategic plan to cut the number of NRL teams back to 12 because, it was suggested, we were running out of top players. If that's the case, after the last Test against Great Britain, I suggest we increase the number of clubs here to 16, bring on more youngsters, rethink the salary cap where clubs are penalised for bringing good young players through the ranks and concentrate on building the NRL competition to even bigger and better things. Clubs are what make rugby league go round. Let's never forget it.

I see nothing wrong in developing a full draft so the smaller and less financial clubs can bring their player power up to strength under the salary cap and when you've got 16 teams, professionally managed and coached, then you've got a competition.

John Monie still finds himself a keen student of the game he's been championing for many years and it is never far from his thoughts or conversation as he reflects on past stars and bright prospects for the future.

Rugby league teams are more and more being driven round the park by formidable half-backs similar to the awesome American football quarter-backs. It's becoming increasingly obvious the best half-backs are worth their weight in gold if your team is going to be a contender for the title. The top half-dozen teams in the 2002 NRL competition had the best halves in my opinion just like St George did many years ago with Billy Smith, Parramatta with Peter Sterling, and Wigan with Andy Gregory.

Only superlatives can describe Joey Johns, Newcastle,

State and Aussie skipper, and hopefully he'll be around showing off his wares for years. The Warriors' man behind the scrum, Stacey Jones, is another brilliant player who joined the Warriors at the beginning when I was coach and played first grade while still only 17.

Though there may be a season left in Alfie Langer he'll always be known as The Bronco Prince to Wally Lewis's King, while Brett Kimmorley is showing at the Sharks the sort of form that took Melbourne's Storm to the premiership. A rising star is the Bulldogs' Brent Sherwin, who is fast developing a true half's trait of taking the ball to the line and off-loading, and Craig Wing showed patches of brilliance and extraordinary speed off the mark while he was serving Sydney Roosters' scrum base. Most of these players will be around for a few years and, almost certainly, the team they play for will be near the top. Newcastle, if Johns stays there, has the added advantage of his unerring boot. Teams without a consistent kicker in today's rugby league will always battle to be at the top.

There are dozens of potential champions coming on tap in Australia and they are the future of the greatest game of all. A standout in my book is the Bulldogs' Braith Anasta, who could be Australian lock or five-eighth for years to come. He's got it all. Attitude under pressure, excellent defence and a competent kicking game. His teammate Willie Mason, shock Test selection, is going to get better and better and at full pace full-backs will find it hard to make him break stride.

Warriors back rower Ali Laultiti, another youngster who came on the scene while I was coach, has developed into the best line breaker and off-loader in the competition. Oppositions will need a gang to stop him.

The Broncos have proved year after year they are the team to beat in Australia and when I coached Wigan in the World Club Championship at Central Park, the Broncos were awesome opponents and beat us soundly. Raging Bull, Gordon Tallis and Darren Lockyer have now emerged as the élite of any national squad. Tallis is the go-to man when the team needs something extra and an opposition red alert goes on whenever Lockyer is within striking distance. Lockyer's ability to glide to the outside of defenders or split the middle is a delight to watch.

Jason Ryles, St George Illawarra's latest addition to the rep ranks, is a tough defender and an aggressive attacker who can advance the ball when seemingly there is nowhere to go, while Trent Barrett is a great athlete who can play five-eighth, centre or lock, a valuable ability in today's game.

Newcastle's Danny Buderis and Steve Simpson are two more players I consider destined for even greater things. Simpson, a second rower built like a front rower, does the tough yards when needed and, in most games, finds himself in the clear at least twice. Buderis is one of the game's better defenders and a dangerous dummy half who can hold the markers and spring the front rowers into space. As for Newcastle's Andrew Johns, there appears nothing on the field of play he can't do better than anyone else.

Monie, whom some may have dubbed the uncompromising coach, shifts a little uneasily by the waters of his canal home. He looks long and hard at the tinnie he uses for checking crab pots, at the golf clubs and the surfboard as he answers the question about what he misses most, leaving the top of the coaching heap.

I've been asked and asked and I've tried to answer honestly every time. But it was just recently, when I went down to a Brisbane–Newcastle game, I found the answer. I don't think I've ever missed the drudgery of everyday training, the travel, the cold and the wet, and the disappointments. But it was at this game I think I finally put my finger on it. It was the buzz. The ground was close to full and the excitement was building well before the kick-off. A great roar went up at the start and it didn't seem to stop till the end. It makes the hair stand up on the back of your neck. That's what I miss.

FACT FILE

- Woy Woy, New South Wales. Captain/coach 1971–72. Won the Grand Final six times – 1975 to 1980 inclusive.
- Parramatta, 1984. First grade coach Monie took the Eels to the Grand Final, losing to Canterbury-Bankstown by 6–4.
- Parramatta, 1986. Monie took the Eels to the Grand Final, beating Canterbury by 4–2.
- Wigan, 1989–93. Head coach and a haul of trophies in four years that can only ever be matched – not beaten. Four times Division One champions. Four times Challenge Cup winners. Regal Trophy winners twice. Premiership winners. Lancashire Cup winners. Charity Shield winners. Coach of the Year 1990–93 and Wigan winning World Club Championship against Penrith at Anfield in 1991. World Sevens winners 1992.
- Auckland, 1995. Monie rejoined a crisis-ridden Wigan club, where he guided his former champions to the Rugby League Cup final and the grand Final. Wigan beat Leeds Rhinos by 10–4, topped the Super League, losing only two games out of 23, and Monie became the first coach to guide sides to win a Grand Final at opposite ends of the world.